101
Activities for Creating Effective Technology Staff Development Programs

A Sourcebook of Games, Stories, Role-Playing, and Learning Exercises for Administrators

101 Activities for Creating Effective Technology Staff Development Programs

A Sourcebook of Games, Stories, Role-Playing, and Learning Exercises for Administrators

by Gerald D. Bailey and Gwen L. Bailey

SCHOLASTIC

LEADERSHIP
POLICY
RESEARCH™

NEW YORK • TORONTO • LONDON • AUCKLAND • SYDNEY

ISBN 0-590-49748-0

12 11 10 9 8 7 6 5 4 3 2 1   1 2 3 2 5/9

Printed in the U.S.A.

Library of Congress Cataloging-in-Publication Data

Bailey, Gerald D.
    101 activities for creating effective technology staff developmnet programs: a sourcebook of games, stories, role-playing, and learning exercises for administrators / Gerald D. Bailey, Gwen L. Bailey.
    by Gerald D. Bailey and Dan Lumley.
        p.   cm.
    Includes bibliographical references.
    ISBN 0-590-49748-0
    1. Educational technology—Handbooks, manuals, etc.
    2. Educational innovations—Handbooks, manuals, etc.
    3. Teachers-Training of—Handbooks, manuals, etc.
I. Bailey, Gwen Lee Cozine.   II. Title.   III. Title: One hundred one activities for creating effective staff development programs.
LB 1028.3.B35 1994
371.3'078—dc20   93–43260
                                                                                                      CIP

TABLE OF CONTENTS □□□□□□□□□□□□□□□□□□□□□□□□□□□□

ACKNOWLEDGMENTS

During the writing of this sourcebook, we have received assistance from numerous individuals. Grateful thanks is given to those principals, central office administrators, technology coordinators, and classroom teachers who participated in the research and development (R&D) testing cycles used to create this book. The activities that follow have been field-tested by highly creative administrators who have spent countless hours as trainers of technology staff development programs.

101 Activities for Creating Effective Technology Staff Development Programs would have never been written without the continual support and encouragement from Lloyd Chilton, Executive Director, Leadership/Policy/Research, Scholastic Inc. We extend our personal gratitude to him.

Finally, we want to acknowledge those countless administrators, technology coordinators, and classroom teachers who have paved the way for the rest of us. Our deepest hope is that this sourcebook will inspire a whole new generation of educators who see themselves as technology leaders.

Gerald D. Bailey & Gwen L. Bailey
Manhattan, Kansas
December 22, 1993

INTRODUCTION □□□□□□□□□□□□□□□□□□□□□□□□□□□□□□□□□□□

101 Activities for Creating Effective Technology Staff Development Programs provides administrators, technology coordinators, and other technology leaders with dozens of games, stories, role playing, and learning activities related to integrating technology into schools. The format of this book is designed for the busy administrator who needs quick, creative, and easy-to-use ideas for technology staff development programs.

SOURCEBOOK ORGANIZATION

This sourcebook is organized like a cookbook and has five stages: (1) Getting Ready for Change and Understanding Technology Staff Development Programs, (2) Planning Your Technology Staff Development Program, (3) Implementing Your Technology Staff Development Program, (4) Institutionalizing Your Technology Staff Development Program, and (5) Special Activities.

Each stage addresses a question as follows:

STAGE #1 What do I need to know prior to starting the program?

STAGE #2 How do I plan for the program?

STAGE #3 How do I conduct the program?

STAGE #4 How do I evaluate the program as well as make the program a permanent fixture of the school organization?

STAGE #5 How do I deal with special problems in each of the previous four stages?

The first four stages are derived from Bailey-Lumley's **Four-Stage Technology Staff Development Model** which is described in greater detail in *Creating a Technology Staff Development Program—A school administrator's sourcebook for redefining teaching and learning using the emerging technologies* (1994). The fifth stage, called Special Activities for Situations and Trainers, contains a variety of activities for both the administrator (trainer) and technology staff development teams.

ACTIVITIES

Within each of the five sections, the sourcebook uses several styles of activities: (1) games, (2) role-playing, (3) stories, and (4) learning exercises, defined as follows:

Games—exercise with a set of rules that lead to a conclusion. Games allow a relaxed and fun way to study a concept. These games are not frivolous, but are designed to evoke an action and conclusion by participants.

Role-Playing—acting out of a character(s) or situation(s) which results in some action or decision. Role-playing exercises are designed to provide a vicarious experience for participants that allow them to practice future experiences. Interaction, empathy, and understanding are strong learning hallmarks of role-playing exercises.

Stories—narration of event or events; a tale related to a learning concept. Stories are used to help participants visualize the concept that is being developed. In addition, storytelling heightens interest and underscores the importance of the concept.

Learning Exercises—event where new or unique information is provided by the leader and then acted on by participants. Learning or informational activities are used to teach concepts by providing new or unique information and then getting the group involved in discussing that information.

ACTIVITY FORMAT

Each activity is usually one page in length and is designed for quick reading. The format of the activity contains six sections: Title, Goal, Focus Question, Strategy, Discussion Questions, and Reference. Each section attempts to answer a specific question for the technology leader when preparing a training session:

Title—What is the name of this activity?

Goal—What is the specific purpose of this technology staff development activity?

Focus Question—What question can be used to help zero in on the issue or problem?

Strategy—What are the specific steps that can be used to lead participants through the technology staff development activity?

Discussion Questions—What questions can be used to stimulate discussion and enhance learning?

Reference—What is or who is the original source of this activity?

BIBLIOGRAPHY

The bibliography is organized around the various stages in the Bailey-Lumley's Four-Stage Technology Staff Development Model (1994). The sectionalized bibliography provides a road map for those technology leaders who desire additional, in-depth information about the activities contained in this sourcebook.

HOW TO USE THIS SOURCEBOOK

Suggestion #1: Don't read this sourcebook from cover to cover. Use it like a cookbook and thumb through the pages to find what you need.

Suggestion #2: Think about a question or problem that you are facing in each of the four technology staff development program stages, then select the activity on the basis of how well it fits your particular need.

Suggestion #3: Find activities that suggest a different way to solve the question or problem you are facing. Stimulate your thinking about the question and problem in a different way by studying a variety of activities which are presented in this sourcebook.

Suggestion #4: Treat the table of contents like the yellow pages in the telephone book. Think about your problem or question, then let your fingers do the walking to find the activity that suits your needs.

Suggestion #5: Don't use these activities as a substitute for in-depth training. The intention of the activities is to stimulate ideas when various problems are identified in the technology staff development program.

Remember, use this sourcebook to make learning fun, both for you and the participants. Use this sourcebook to make your technology staff development program a unique experience—a program that participants enjoy and rave about. Keep them involved! Keep them stimulated! Keep them laughing! But most importantly, keep them excited about reinventing teaching and learning with the emerging technologies!

STAGE 1

Preparing for Change and Understanding Technology Staff Development Programs

Diagnosing Your Technology User Level

GOAL

▶ To allow participants to diagnose their technology user style.

FOCUS QUESTIONS

▶ In relation to the emerging technologies, how would you classify yourself as a technology user?

▶ Why is it important to know participants' user levels?

STRATEGY

Provide the following information:

1. There are potentially five types of technology users that could be placed in learning teams: I. High-End User, II. Moderate User, III. Low-End User, IV. Non-User, and V. Technophobe. Every potential learning team has different users. Yet many technology staff development programs never acknowledge the skill differences among these people. That is, everybody gets the same information and training irrespective of level of competence and attitudes toward the emerging technologies. Diagnosing user levels can be helpful when thinking about possible training team combinations, as well as providing opportunities to meet individual needs and abilities in the entire technology staff development program. The levels are defined as follows:

   I. High-End User—person on the leading edge of technology; knows much about emerging technologies; usually experiments with technology-based learning methods.

   II. Moderate User—person who makes use of available technology, but not deeply immersed in technology-based learning methodologies.

   III. Low-End User—person who makes limited use of emerging technologies.

   IV. Non-User—person who does not make use of the emerging technologies in learning activities.

   V. Technophobe—person who fears, hates, despises, or distrusts the emerging technologies.

2. Using the user identification form (see next page), indicate what user group you belong to and explain why you feel that way.

3. Discuss and explain your self-diagnosis to your team members.

DISCUSSION QUESTIONS

▶ Why is it important to have an understanding of technology user levels?

▶ How can this information be used to plan your technology staff development program? Organize learning activities? Group team members?

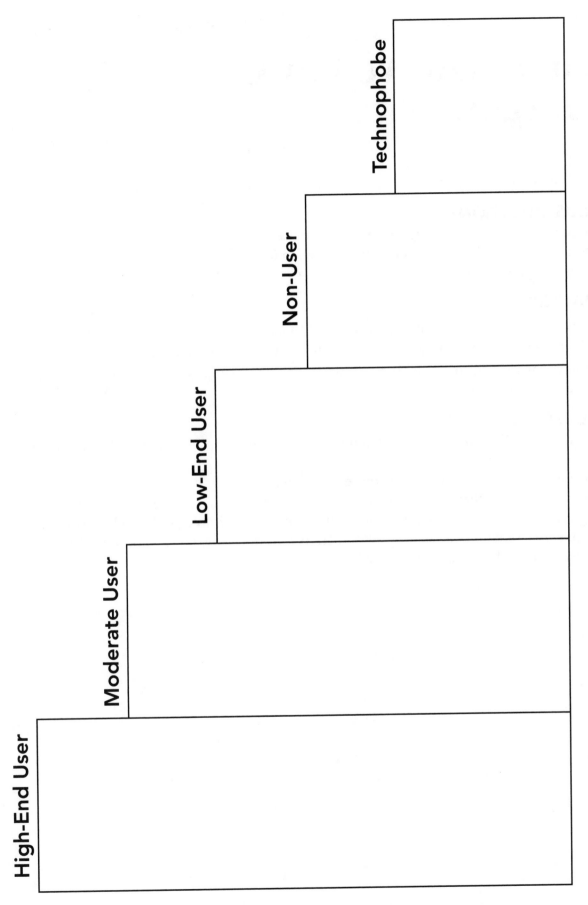

What Kind of Technology User Are You?

Where Do We Put Our Energies?

GOAL

▶ To explore where schools should place their emphasis on the emerging technologies.

FOCUS QUESTIONS

▶ How should the emerging technologies be used in schools?

▶ How should priorities be set by schools when looking at the potential uses of the emerging technologies?

STRATEGY

1. Review the summary sheet (see next page) to familiarize yourself with the Emerging Technologies Classifications. Then circulate information among participants.

2. Allow participants to discuss their ideas about how the emerging technologies should be used in their school.

DISCUSSION QUESTIONS

▶ How should a school or district determine priorities about how to use the emerging technologies?

▶ How have other schools made these decisions?

▶ Is it important that technology leaders and technology staff development teams give consideration to the potential uses of the emerging technologies? In other words, is one area of emphasis, such as administrative productivity, more important than teaching and learning? Why or why not?

Where Do We Put Our Energies?: Emerging Technologies Classifications

1. Administrative Productivity

inventory, purchasing, employee records, payroll, public communication, student progress, student attendance, student records, district/school/staff communication via e-mail, networked buildings, etc.

2. Teaching-Learning

Hypermedia, multimedia, electronic cooperative learning, electronic simulation, Integrated Learning Systems (ILSs), networking (e.g., classrooms, computer labs, etc.), distance learning, technology education learning/technology preparation learning (i.e., vocational)

3. Curriculum Management

electronic card catalog, computerized circulation, electronic curriculum materials, etc.

4. Electronic Retrieval/Storage

laser videodisc, CD-ROM, videotape, computer floppies, computer hard drive, etc. used for retrieving and storing information

5. School Restructuring/Transformation

microcomputer, mainframe, etc. used to engage in school improvement programs, etc. (e.g., any use of the technology to radically redefine teaching, learning, and the concept now known as schools)

Paradigm Shift

GOAL

▶ To illustrate the meaning of paradigm shift and how it applies to thinking about technology staff development programs.

FOCUS QUESTIONS

▶ What is a paradigm?

▶ What is a paradigm shift?

▶ How can paradigms help us understand the role of the emerging technologies in teaching and learning? In school restructuring/school transformation?

STRATEGY

1. A common problem for newcomers to the emerging technologies is understanding how the emerging technologies have impacted our world. Many experts believe that the emerging technologies have caused a paradigm shift in all aspects of society—military, business, and leisure. This paradigm shift is often illustrated by referring to the industrial era being replaced by the Information-Age. To illustrate this paradigm shift, Barker's principles of paradigms can be both provocative and motivating. Share the information about paradigms with participants (see next page).

DISCUSSION QUESTION

▶ How can the concept of paradigm shift help explain the need for technology staff development programs that will facilitate schools who want to move into the 21st century—the Information Age?

REFERENCE

Adapted from Barker, J.A. (1992). *Future Edge—Discovering the New Paradigms of Success.* New York: Morrow.

□□□

Seven Principles of the New Paradigm Profile

Paradigm defined—a set of rules and regulations (written or unwritten) that does two things: (1) establishes or defines boundaries, and (2) tells you how to behave inside the boundaries in order to be successful.

Paradigm Shift defined—a change to a new game, a new set of rules.

Paradigm Shift illustration—industrial era replaced by Information Age; muscle was the tool of the industrial era and information has become the tool of the Information Age.

When a paradigm shift occurs:

1. Everything goes back to zero.

2. Everything is challenged.

3. Previous successes guarantee nothing.

4. Previous experiences and knowledge blind us to new ideas.

5. New rules and regulations must be put into effect.

6. New paradigms come from outside.

7. New paradigms leaders have trust in their judgment.

> *"A paradigm shift takes about 25 years to occur . . . because the original defenders have to die off."*
>
> —Thomas S. Kuhn,
> *The Structure of Scientific Revolution*

Adapted from Barker, J.A. (1992). *Future Edge—Discovering the New Paradigms of Success.* New York: Morrow.

Predictions from History

GOAL

▶ To illustrate that existing needs and new technology have caused radical change throughout history while ridiculous predictions to the contrary have been prevalent—even when "experts" have made them.

FOCUS QUESTION

▶ What predictions were proven to be wrong in the history of the western world?

STRATEGY

1. Relate the following predictions in recent history:

"Why, sir, would you make a ship sail against the wind and currents by lighting a bonfire under her deck? I pray you excuse me. I have no time to listen to such nonsense."
Napoléon Bonaparte, emperor of France, to Robert Fulton

"There is nothing left to invent."
Director of U.S. Patent Office, 1875

"Airplanes are interesting toys, but they have no military value."
Marshal Ferdinand Foch, 1911

"Who the hell wants to hear actors talk."
Harry M. Warner, 1927

"Whatever happens, the U.S. Navy is not going to be caught napping."
Frank Knox, U.S. Secretary of the Navy, December 4, 1941

"With over 50 foreign cars already on sale here, the Japanese auto industry isn't likely to carve out a big slice of the U.S. market."
Business Week, 1958

"Space travel is utter bilge."
Sir Richard van der Riet Wooley, The Astronomer Royal, 1956

2. Ask participants about other predictions that they remember.

3. Then relate one more prediction:

"The emerging technologies will never transform education."
—Anonymous

4. Engage participants in discussion.

DISCUSSION QUESTIONS

▶ Why have there been so many predictions that have proven to be false?
▶ Why has technology had such a profound impact on societal change?
▶ How can these predictions help us put the emerging technologies in perspective?
▶ Why is it difficult to predict change when technological innovations are at the core of change?

REFERENCE

Boone, L.E. (1992). *Quotable Business.* New York: Random House.

Predictions About the Future: From 1893 to 1993

GOAL
▶ To provide an opportunity to think about the future.

FOCUS QUESTION
▶ In 1883, what did futurists predict about 1993?

STRATEGY
Relate the following story:

1. In 1893, 74 prominent Americans wrote essays about what life would be like in 1993. Newspapers published these essays as part of a promotion for the World's Columbian Exposition, which opened in Chicago, May 1893. Sample forecasts from 1893 were:

    "The railroad will still be the fastest means of travel."
    —Charles Foster, Treasury Secretary

    ". . .mail in 1993 will still travel by stagecoach and horseback rider."
    —John Wanamaker, Postmaster General

2. Identify and discuss other **incorrect** predictions which include:
    ▶ The price of postage will be reduced to 1 cent.
    ▶ Life span of 150 years will be common.
    ▶ Transcontinental mail would be transmitted in pneumatic tubes.
    ▶ Laws will be so simplified that there will be no work for lawyers.
    ▶ All forests will be gone, so builders will have to use stone, iron, and other materials.
    ▶ There will be little crime because criminals will be prevented from breeding.
    ▶ Religion will solve the alcohol problems.

3. Identify and discuss other **correct predictions**:
    ▶ Homes will be air-conditioned.
    ▶ Florida will boom as a leisure state.
    ▶ Cities will become groups of suburbs.

4. Have participants list five predictions for 2093. Exchange predictions and discuss implications for technology staff development programs.

DISCUSSION QUESTIONS
▶ What can we learn from past predictions that apply to the future?
▶ Why can't we predict the future very well?

REFERENCE
Adapted from Walter, D. (1992). *American's Best Minds Look 100 Years Into the Future on the Occasion of the 1893 World's Columbian Exposition.* New York: American & World Geographic Publishing.

□□

Predictions About the Emerging Technologies and Education by 2020

GOAL
▶ To provide an opportunity to think about the future and how teaching and learning will be impacted by the emerging technologies.

FOCUS QUESTION
▶ What will teaching, learning, and schools look like by the year 2020?

STRATEGY

1. Distribute the prediction quiz (see next page).

2. Provide oral directions about the scale, which consists of three areas: likelihood, impact, and expertise.

3. Allow participants to complete the quiz and then relate their predictions to each other.

4. Share the following: Predicting the future is difficult for several reasons:
   ▶ Changes occur constantly around the world, and we are not very aware of them.
   ▶ Recent events dominate our thinking about the future.
   ▶ The pace of society and technology is phenomenal, and we are not able to see how one event may impact other events.

5. Engage participants in discussion about predictions and the emerging technologies.

DISCUSSION QUESTIONS
▶ Why was or why wasn't there a wide range of opinions?
▶ How can this prediction quiz help us understand the future?
▶ Why can't we predict the future very well?
▶ What can we predict about the emerging technologies?

REFERENCE
Adapted from Cornish, E. (1993). The futurist poll, *The Futurist, 27* (3), 43.

Predictions About the Emerging Technologies and Education by 2020

Directions: Consider the following predictions. Rank each event's likelihood of occurring on a scale from 1 to 10 (1= unlikely to occur, 10=likely to occur). Then rank the event's potential impact on teaching, learning, schools, society, etc. (1=definitely won't happen or "no impact," 10=definitely will happen or "has significant impact"). In addition, rank your own expertise on each subject (1=just guessing; 2=some knowledge; 3=well informed; 4=expert).

Prediction	Likelihood (1–10)	Impact (1–10)	Expertise (1–4)
1. Technology-based learning methods will replace teacher-centered instruction.	_____	_____	_____
2. Technology will revolutionize every aspect of work, leisure, and learning.	_____	_____	_____
3. Smart medicine (i.e., pills) will revolutionize how people learn.	_____	_____	_____
4. Learning in schools will be replaced by learning anywhere, anytime, anyplace.	_____	_____	_____
5. Computers will be cheap, plentiful, as well as allow access to any information throughout the world.	_____	_____	_____
6. Learning how to learn will be more important than basic knowledge in the school curriculum.	_____	_____	_____
7. Written texts will be replaced by electronic curriculum sources (e.g., databases, electronic repository, etc.).	_____	_____	_____
8. Team-oriented learning will replace most individual or independent learning.	_____	_____	_____
9. Most learning experiences will be intergenerational (i.e., people of all ages studying similar problems).	_____	_____	_____
10. Business and schools will form partnerships to create work-site classes for children of the workers.	_____	_____	_____

Futurists

GOAL

▶ To familiarize participants with information that has a direct bearing on the need for technology staff development programs in schools.

FOCUS QUESTIONS

▶ How is society changing and what role is technology going to play in the 21st century?

▶ What are demographers and futurists telling us about the future?

STRATEGY

Knowledge about the future and current trends in business and industry have a direct bearing on the focus and direction of technology staff development programs.

1. To begin to familiarize participants with current and future trends, circulate the audit on the next page.

2. Direct participants to take the audit (see next page), entitled The Emerging Technologies and Public Education.

3. Have participants share their reactions to the audit with each other.

4. Add additional demographic or futurist information to the six items and discuss the implications for schools in the next decade.

DISCUSSION QUESTIONS

▶ How much of this information was familiar to you?

▶ Can this information be used to point a direction for schools and does it underscore the importance of technology in teaching and learning?

REFERENCE

Adapted from (1993). *Georgia Center Quarterly(8)*, 2.

The Emerging Technologies and Public Education

Did You Know . . .

____Yes ____No **1.** . . . that IBM has awarded grants of up to $3 million each to nine universities, including Georgia Tech, with the goal of improving the teaching and practice of total quality management (TQM).

____Yes ____No **2.** . . . that by the year 2000, IBM and Ford Motor Company will have moved significantly toward the delivery of education and training through technology; that only 25 percent of employee training will take place in IBM classrooms and only 50 percent in Ford classrooms?

____Yes ____No **3.** . . . that in this decade, "quality time" will become a status symbol and a luxury item; most Americans agree that having free time is just as important as making money?

____Yes ____No **4.** . . . that by the year 2010, demographers predict ethnic minorities will constitute about one third of the U.S. population and that in some states, including California, the minority race will be white?

____Yes ____No **5.** . . . that in a study of U.S. organizations with 100 or more employees, 19 percent of the organizations provide workers with remedial (the three R's) training?

How well did you do?

Count your yeses. If you got:

   5—You are Information-Age literate.

   4—You are very knowledgeable.

   3—Not bad!

   2—Just about average.

   1—You don't read much demographic and futurist literature.

   0—Whoa! You're in for a big shock about the future of this country!

Remember Your First Technological Wonder?

GOAL

▶ To illustrate that technology staff development committee members have similar and different memories of technological advancements and events depending on their age.

FOCUS QUESTION

▶ What technological advancement impressed you most?

STRATEGY

Remember when something really impressed you as whiz-bang? We can tell a lot about each other by what we remember as monumental events in our lives.

1. Have participants write technological advancements that they remember at different points in their lives.

WHAT TECHNOLOGICAL ADVANCEMENT IMPRESSED YOU MOST. . .

Age Level	*Technology Example*
▶ **Early Childhood**	_____
▶ **Teenager**	_____
▶ **Young Adult**	_____
▶ **Current Age**	_____

---

2. In small groups, allow participants to share their stories with each other.

DISCUSSION QUESTIONS

▶ What do these stories say about us as individuals?
▶ What do these stories say about very young people?
▶ What age group *has seen* the greatest changes in their lifetime?
▶ What age group *will see* the greatest technological changes in their lifetime?

My Technology Cup Runneth Over

GOAL

▶ To show the importance of an open-minded approach when dealing with the emerging technologies.

FOCUS QUESTION

▶ Why is it important to be mentally ready to take on a new challenge such as integrating technology into teaching and learning?

STRATEGY

Tell the group the following story:

An old Japanese master invited a hopeful student to his home for tea. Upon the student's arrival, nervousness prompted the student to talk at length about his experiences, accomplishments, and adventures. After a rather long unidirectional dialogue by the student, the Japanese master asked the student if he would like a cup of tea.

The student replied, "Yes."

As the Japanese master poured the tea into the cup, it overflowed, spilling over the rim and consequently the saucer. The master continued to pour as if nothing unusual was happening. Finally, unable to ignore the incident, the student exclaimed, "Sir, the tea is spilling over the rim."

"Yes," said the Japanese master, "you are much like this cup. You are so filled with your own importance, how can I teach you anything until you first empty your cup?"

DISCUSSION QUESTIONS

▶ Do you identify with the hopeful student?
▶ How can we get mentally ready for technology staff development programs?

Defining Moments

GOAL

▶ To illustrate the importance of personal action and commitment which are based on dramatic events in leaders' lives.

FOCUS QUESTIONS

▶ What events in your life have had great impact on you?

▶ What events (related to technology) have had the greatest impact on your work with technology?

STRATEGY

Relate the following information and story:

1. Many people have had experiences that have left a profound impact on their personal and professional lives. Brent Filson describes these as "defining moments." He calls them a "naked, wonderful instant in time that changes you forever." Filson's own "defining moment" was a dramatic one.

2. He tells the following story about an executive:

   Our squad was ambushed by the Vietcong. Every man in the unit was killed except him. From the hiding place that had preserved his life, he watched the Vietcong move away into the jungle. Suddenly, the last Communist soldier in line turned and looked him right in the eye.

   "All he had to do was pull the trigger and I was dead," said the executive. "But then he did something that astonished me. He turned away and kept on walking. He gave me my life. Because of that moment, all the years since, every day I give as much as I can to people."

3. Then provide the following information:

   That story was a real dramatic defining moment! We all have them! People who relate defining moments to others can have an impact on others. But they must be action oriented, highly visual, brief, and directly related to your message.

4. Then allow participants to share defining moments in their lives.

DISCUSSION QUESTIONS

▶ Describe the defining moments that have had a dramatic impact on your life.

▶ Who has had a defining moment which was related to the emerging technologies? Share your story with the rest of the group.

▶ Why are defining moments important to people working with the emerging technologies?

REFERENCE

Adapted from Filson, B. (1992). *Defining Moment: Motivating People to Take Action.* Williamstown, MA: Williamstown Publishers.

Why We Can't Change!

GOAL

▶ To illustrate that there are dozens of reasons why change is difficult or won't work in the minds of many people.

FOCUS QUESTIONS

▶ Why is change so difficult?

▶ Why do we always have so many reasons not to change?

STRATEGY

1. Divide participants into small groups.

2. Ask them to identify a top-ten list of reasons why any kind of change—especially technology and technology staff development programs—won't work.

3. Then circulate Fifty Reasons Why We/It/They Can't Change (see next page).

4. Compare and discuss the two lists.

DISCUSSION QUESTIONS

▶ Which reasons are valid? Not valid? Why?

▶ Why are there so many reasons change cannot happen?

▶ How can we help people overcome these negative reactions to change?

RESOURCE

Adapted from Boone, L. E. (1992). *Quotable Business—Over 2,500 Funny, Irreverent, and Insightful Quotations About Corporate Life*. New York: Random House.

Fifty Reasons Why We/It/They Can't Change

1. We've never done it before.

2. Nobody else has ever done it.

3. It has never been tried before.

4. We tried it before a few years back.

5. Another school has tried it before.

6. We've been doing it this way for 25 years.

7. It won't work in a small school.

8. It won't work in a large school.

9. It won't work in our school.

10. Why change—it's working okay.

11. The superintendent will never buy it.

12. The board of education will never buy it.

13. The parents will never buy it.

14. Other schools are not doing it.

15. It is too much trouble to change.

16. Our school is different.

17. The janitor says it can't be done.

18. It can't be done.

19. We don't have the money.

20. We don't have the necessary staff development.

21. We don't have the equipment.

22. The union will scream.

23. It's too far out there—too futuristic.

24. I am too close to retirement. You can't teach an old dog new tricks.

25. It's too radical of a change.

26. It's beyond my responsibility.

27. It's not my job.

28. We don't have the time.

29. It will replace teachers.

30. There is no research to support it.

31. You can prove anything with research.

32. Students won't buy it.

33. It's contrary to school policy.

34. It's too expensive.

35. It's not our problem.

36. I don't like it.

37. You're right, but . . .

38. They didn't teach us this stuff in undergraduate school.

39. We're not ready for it.

40. It needs more thought.

41. Administrators won't accept it.

42. We can't take the chance.

43. We'd need support from business and industry.

44. We're doing all right as it is.

45. A committee study needs to be done.

46. Students won't learn as much.

47. This isn't very well thought out.

48. This is another hair-brain idea from "pointy-headed" university professors.

49. It's impossible.

50. It's just another fad — you know, just "this year's new thing."

20

Having an Edge

GOAL

▶ To show how some people can anticipate change—a quality that gives them an edge over other people who do not anticipate change.

FOCUS QUESTIONS

▶ Why do some people have the ability to anticipate change?

▶ What advantage does this give them?

STRATEGY

Relate the following story:

1. Think about the great athletes in America today. What makes them great? Wayne Gretzky is arguably the greatest hockey player in history. Asked about his secret for continuing to lead the National Hockey League in goals year after year, Gretzky replied, "I skate to where the puck is going to be, not where it has been."

2. Invite participant reactions to Gretzky's statement.

3. Allow participants to identify other great athletes from basketball, football, baseball, etc. Ask if these athletes have the same quality that Gretzky seems to possess?

DISCUSSION QUESTIONS

▶ What are the implications of Gretzky's answer for technology leaders?

▶ Do educators, politicians, and business leaders have this same skill?

▶ Why is having an edge a significant leadership skill?

RESOURCE

Adapted from Boone, L.E. (1992). *Quotable Business—Over 2,500 funny, Irreverent, and Insightful Quotations About Corporate Life*. New York: Random House, p. 299.

People Who Bring Change

GOAL

▶ To illustrate the different types of people who bring change to organizations or cause paradigm shifts.

FOCUS QUESTION

▶ Who brings change to the organization? How can you capitalize on these people when integrating emerging technologies into education?

STRATEGY

Relate the following:

1. According to Joel Barker, there are four categories of people who precipitate change in an organization (or cause a paradigm shift). They include: (a) a young person fresh out of training (novice), (b) an older person shifting fields (expert who applies expertise to new field), (c) a maverick (a rule breaker), (d) tinkerer (one who solves problems).

   a. The new person brings about change because he or she is unfamiliar. He doesn't know it can't be done. He doesn't know any different so he navigates without knowing it cannot be done. Historical example: Albert Einstein and his scientific theories at an early age.

   b. The expert shifting fields brings previous knowledge to a new field. These people apply their previous insights to problems in distinctly different fields. Historical example: W.C. Demming and his ideas of Total Quality Management.

   c. The maverick is a change buster. Historical example: Steven Spielberg and his innovative style of movies.

   d. The tinkerer sees problem solving as a daily activity and can't go on until problems are solved. Historical examples: Leonardo da Vinci and Thomas Edison.

2. Ask participants to list other historical examples of paradigm shifters.

3. Ask participants if they could put themselves into any of these four categories.

4. Ask if anyone could put their friends or associates into one or more of these categories.

DISCUSSION QUESTIONS

▶ Is it helpful to think about your associates in terms of these four groups of people?
▶ Are you a paradigm shifter in your school? In your technology staff development program?

REFERENCE

Adapted from Barker, J.A. (1992). *Future Shift—Discovering the New Paradigms of Success*. New York: Morrow.

Seven Signs of Change Arthritis

GOAL

▶ To illustrate that many people in education and society suffer from change arthritis.

FOCUS QUESTION

▶ What are the seven signs of change arthritis and how can we prevent it from crippling the potential of the technology staff development program?

STRATEGY

1. Circulate the audit dealing with the seven signs of change arthritis to participants (see next page).

2. Allow participants to discuss the audit among themselves.

3. Solicit personal testimonies from participants about whether they have signs of change arthritis.

4. Have participants develop a personal written plan that deals with preventing or dealing with change arthritis.

DISCUSSION QUESTIONS

▶ Can we prevent change arthritis?

▶ If we cannot prevent change arthritis, how do we learn to deal with it?

Do You Have Change Arthritis?

____Yes ____No **1.** Swelling in one or more synapses of your brain when you hear the word change.

____Yes ____No **2.** Early morning mental stiffness when hearing the morning news talking about the speed of change in our society.

____Yes ____No **3.** Recurring pain or tenderness when colleagues or experts use words like *paradigm shift, school transformation, reinventing schools, reinventing government,* etc.

____Yes ____No **4.** Inability to quickly move from one subject to another without fear or panic.

____Yes ____No **5.** Automatic rejection of new ways of looking at persistent problems.

____Yes ____No **6.** Inability to accept change as something positive and constructive.

____Yes ____No **7.** Chronic defensiveness and crabbiness when an outsider has a unique or revolutionary idea about your field or area of expertise.

Scoring: If you said yes to four or more of these questions, you have early signs of change arthritis. If you said yes to three or fewer of these questions, you are probably adaptable to change and will survive the 21st century. Remember, symptoms persisting for more than two weeks could lead to a lifetime of change arthritis.

Resistance to Technology

GOAL

▶ To illustrate that new ideas—especially emerging technologies— are not always easily accepted.

FOCUS QUESTION

▶ How do people of authority and initial users of technology react to new ideas?

STRATEGY

Relate the following stories:

1. Albert Einstein was a young physicist finishing his paper for his Ph.D. When he submitted his dissertation, it was initially rejected. Why? Because when he was working in the patent office, he had taken the opportunity to type his thesis on a typewriter, and his German committee members initially rejected it because they said it should be written in longhand or it would have no professional value.

   and

   The *Adventures of Tom Sawyer* was the first novel ever to be written on a typewriter. It was typed on a Remington in 1875 by Mark Twain himself. Twain, however, wished to withhold the fact. He did not want to write testimonials, he said, or answer questions concerning the operation of the "new-fangled thing."

2. Allow participants to discuss the implications of these stories for technology staff development programs.

DISCUSSION QUESTIONS

▶ Why are people of authority and expertise resistant to change?

▶ Why are people afraid of new technology?

▶ Why are people (like Mark Twain) hesitant or even resistant to talk about technological changes?

▶ How can you use this information to deal with change in your technology staff development program?

We've Always Done It This Way!

GOAL

▶ To get technology leaders to challenge traditions and everyday practices.

FOCUS QUESTION

▶ Why is it important to challenge our time-honored personal habits?

STRATEGY

Share the following story:

1. There is a story about the woman who cuts off the end of the roast before she cooks it. Her husband watches this for years. He asks why she does that, and she says, "Well, that's the way you cook a roast. That's the way my mother did it."

   One day he asks his mother-in-law why she cuts the end of the roast. "I don't know," she says. "My mother did it that way."

   He goes to see the grandmother and asks, "Why did you cut off the end of the roast?"

   She says, "Because it wouldn't fit into my short pan." And so, much of practice evolves because Grandma had a short pan.

2. Allow participants to analyze the meaning of the story, the connection to change, and the use of emerging technologies in teaching and learning.

3. Determine if any participants have similar stories.

DISCUSSION QUESTIONS

▶ What can we learn from this story?
▶ Why do we establish patterns of behavior without giving them much thought?
▶ How often do we challenge our own way of doing things?
▶ What are the implications of this story for how we teach and what we use to teach with?

RESOURCE

Adapted from, Warshaw, M. (1993). The mind style of the entrepreneur, *Success(40)* 3, 28–33.

Cutting Lettuce

GOAL

▶ To get technology leaders to challenge traditions and everyday practices.

FOCUS QUESTION

▶ Is it important to challenge our standard operating procedures?

STRATEGY

Share the following story:

1. There is a true story about the woman who had two daughters and the way they were taught how to cut lettuce for the meal. The mother had always instructed her daughters to remove the stem (the light-colored portion of the lettuce head) because it was bitter. The daughters never questioned the instructions and did what they were told.

   Approximately 20 years later, they were preparing food for a family reunion. At the sink, the grandmother, mother, and granddaughters were preparing lettuce in the same fashion that they always did. When the granddaughters were about to remove the stem of the lettuce, the grandmother remarked, "Don't throw the stem away. It is very sweet and good to eat." The granddaughters and mother were very shocked. "But why?" the mother said. "You always told us to prepare it that way." The grandmother replied, "Well, that is what my mother told me, but I just discovered last month that it is very sweet. You should try it."

2. Allow participants to analyze the meaning of the story, the connection to change, and the use of emerging technologies in teaching and learning.

3. Determine if any participants have similar stories.

DISCUSSION QUESTIONS

▶ What can we learn from this story?
▶ Why do we establish patterns of behavior without giving them much thought?
▶ How often do we challenge our own way of doing things?
▶ What are the implications of this story for how we teach and what we teach with?

Old Habits Die Hard

GOAL

▶ To show one's innate resistance to change or to being changed.

FOCUS QUESTION

▶ Why is it difficult for us to change?

STRATEGY

1. Ask the group to take off their shoes.

2. Tell them to put them back on—and remember which shoe they put on first.

3. Then ask them to take them off again.

4. Now ask them to put them on again, only in reverse order. (If they put the right shoe on first, put the left shoe on first, and vice versa.)

5. Now engage participants in discussion about their personal feelings concerning change.

6. Additional alternatives to routine behaviors which might be explored:
   a. Putting your earrings on (women).
   b. Putting your billfold in the opposite pocket (men).

DISCUSSION QUESTIONS

▶ Did you find the change awkward?

▶ How did this change make you feel?

▶ If even this slight physical change may have some built-in resistance, what implications does this have for more substantial intellectual change, such as using the emerging technologies to transform education?

Pick a Corner!

GOAL

▶ To get participants to think about where they stand in relation to innovations.

FOCUS QUESTION

▶ Does innovative thinking remain constant for individuals on all issues and innovations?

STRATEGY

1. Before the session begins, identify an innovation that has occurred in the last five or ten years. Ask the group to divide themselves in the four corners of the room with these subsets:
   ▶ Were you a leader in implementing this innovation?
   ▶ Were you one of the last to accept this innovation?
   ▶ Were you somewhere in between?
   ▶ You still don't accept this innovation.

2. Ask participants the following questions:
   ▶ What did they like or dislike about their respective places during this innovation?
   ▶ What were their feelings during the process of being first, middle, or last during this innovation? How did others treat them?
   ▶ In retrospect, would they have preferred to be in a different place as it relates to this innovation?

3. After each group has 10 to 15 minutes to discuss these questions, ask one person to report for each group.

4. Now ask the group to rearrange themselves according to how they stand on issues of integrating technology in their school or school district and in technology staff development programs.
   Move to the corner if you are:
   ▶ an innovator promoting and using technology,
   ▶ one of the last persons to accept technology,
   ▶ somewhere in between,
   ▶ still not accepting technology.

DISCUSSION QUESTIONS

▶ How many of you changed corners?
▶ Do people who are traditionally innovators feel equally comfortable with the emerging technologies?

Where Are Your Feet Planted?

GOAL

▶ To get technology leaders to question how important idea people are to organizational change and progress.

FOCUS QUESTIONS

▶ Have you ever been accused of having impractical ideas?

▶ How do we typically react to people who have new and different ideas?

STRATEGY

Tell the following story:

1. Henry Ford once hired an efficiency expert to analyze his automobile operations. The consultant gave the company a good rating, but had doubts about one employee. "It's that man down the corridor," he said. "Every time I go by his office, he's just sitting there with his feet on his desk. He's wasting your money."

   "That man," replied Ford, "once had an idea that saved us millions of dollars. At the time, I believe his feet were planted right where they are now."

2. Get participant reactions to the story.

DISCUSSION QUESTIONS

▶ Why are idea people important to organizations?

▶ How do we typically treat people who have different ideas than our own?

▶ Why do we often accuse idea people of having their feet planted firmly in the air?

▶ Why are some leaders more accepting of people with conventional ideas than of those with different ideas?

The Speed of Change

GOAL
▶ To get participants thinking about the fast pace of technological innovation and its relationship to the change process.

FOCUS QUESTION
▶ How fast is the speed of change?

STRATEGY

1. Allow participants to list as many technologies or emerging technologies that have been used in the United States or the world since 19__ . (pick a date)

2. Place these items on a flip chart. Don't judge if they are right or wrong, and let the group make the determination of correctness.

3. Then, after the list is created, ask participants the following question: Which of these innovations has occurred since 19__? (moving the date closer to the present while placing a check mark next to these innovations)

5. Then move the date up five more years. Ask: Which of these technological innovations have occurred since 19__? Place an *x* next to these.

6. After the group has completed this exercise, explain that by the year 2000, people will see more changes and innovations than we have seen in all of history.

DISCUSSION QUESTIONS
▶ Were you surprised by what we found?
▶ How fast does change occur?
▶ What are the implications of this activity for schools and our technology staff development program?

Environmental Scan

GOAL

▶ To show that massive changes in our society will occur in only a few short years, and these massive changes are being driven by the emerging technologies.

FOCUS QUESTIONS

▶ How fast are things changing?

▶ How are these changes going to impact the way people learn and communicate?

STRATEGY

1. Have students complete the audit (see next page).

2. Discuss participants' responses. (All answers to the ten statements are True.)

3. Allow students to speculate about the impact of the emerging technologies on teaching and learning.

DISCUSSION QUESTIONS

▶ Is any of the information (audit) new to you?

▶ Does any of the information shock you?

▶ Does the future look scary or does it look exciting?

RESOURCE

Adapted from: (Spring 1993). *Georgia Center Quarterly 80*, (3), 6.

Environmental Scan

____T ____F **1.** Case Western University in Georgia is pushing to develop higher education's most advanced learning environment by using a fiber-optic system that will link all student, faculty, and staff computers to each other and to local, national, and international networks.

____T ____F **2.** Mind Extension University beams college credit courses to 36,000 students nationwide under the aegis of such established institutions as the University of Minnesota and Pennsylvania State University.

____T ____F **3.** The multimedia revolution, combining computer text, graphics, sound, animation, and full-motion film and video is well underway and will be a hallmark of the schools and colleges of tomorrow.

____T ____F **4.** The Edison Project (i.e., private school venture) calls for its students to have a "learning partner" both at home and at school, consisting of a monitor, computer, printer, VCR, fax, paint board, stereo, and telephone; this setup will provide unlimited student access to an astonishingly rich library of books, films, speeches, and thousands of learning games.

____T ____F **5.** Currently, some 6,000 public and private on-line services (supporting more than 40,000 bulletin boards) are used monthly by at least two million Americans.

____T ____F **6.** By the year 2000, personal computers could outnumber children in U.S. households.

____T ____F **7.** A goal of Project Gutenberg is to distribute a trillion electronic copies from a collection of 10,000 books through computer networks by 2001.

____T ____F **8.** Today's personal computer will be hopelessly outdated by the end of the decade; keyboards are on the way out and voice-activated computing is on the way in; there is an imminent explosion of pen-based computers (also known as tablet-and-notebook PCs, stylus computers, and electronic slates).

____T ____F **9.** Huge amounts of information will be stored on tiny holograms, permitting retrieval of data in a few seconds or less.

____T ____F **10.** Many see "a great leap in learning" by the mid-21st century; "highly advanced computers will serve as both tutors and libraries, interacting with students individually and giving them access to information" that will dwarf today's Library of Congress holdings; education's formal rigidity will be replaced by customized instruction for students.

Adapted from: (Spring 1993). *Georgia Center Quarterly 8* (3), 6.

What Kind of Risk-Taker Are You?

GOAL

▶ To illustrate that new ideas are not always easily accepted, irrespective of whether it is new technologies, new inventions, or new ideas.

FOCUS QUESTIONS

▶ How do people react to new ideas?

▶ Why do people fear risk-taking and risk takers?

STRATEGY

1. Relate the following historical events:

▶ An irate banker demanded that Alexander Graham Bell remove "that toy" from his office.

▶ A Hollywood producer scrawled a rejection note on a manuscript that became *Gone With the Wind*.

▶ Henry Ford's largest original investor sold out all his stock in 1906.

▶ Roebuck sold out to Sears for $25,000 in 1895. Today, Sears sells $25,000 of goods in 16 seconds.

▶ In 1989–90, after only eight months, David Jackson sold his interest in ETS World Wide Conferencing to his partner Ben P. Cascio. In a few short months (1992), ETS's revenues were $1.4 million.

2. Allow participants to react to the historical information.

3. Ask participants for additional examples.

DISCUSSION QUESTIONS

▶ Why are people resistant to change?

▶ Why are people afraid of risks? Risk-takers?

▶ Why is it difficult for us to see the long-term consequences of our actions and events?

▶ Why are the emerging technologies forcing us to come to grips with risk-taking and innovation?

John Q. Public's Perceptions About Education

GOAL

▶ To familiarize participants with public perception of schools and to understand how emerging technologies fit into this perception.

FOCUS QUESTION

▶ How does the public feel about public education?

STRATEGY

1. Share the information sheet entitled, "What's Wrong with Our Schools?" (see next page).

2. After participants have had a chance to reflect on the information, brainstorm how public perception differs from teachers' and administrators' perceptions.

3. Continue discussion about how the public views the emerging technologies and its potential to impact teaching and learning.

DISCUSSION QUESTIONS

▶ Did the results shock you? Why or why not?

▶ Did the results agree with your own perceptions? Why or why not?

▶ Does it surprise you that no mention of technology or technology-based learning was made? Why or why not?

▶ Do the results surprise you in that no mention was made of the world of work and the school's role to prepare students for work? Why or why not?

REFERENCE

Adapted from Mark Clements, "What's Wrong with Our Schools?," *Parade Magazine*, May 16, 1993.

What's Wrong With Our Schools?

1. 63 percent of Americans rate the quality of public education as poor or fair, while 37 percent rated the schools as good or excellent.

2. 79 percent think there should be a moment of silence during school when children can pray if they want to.

3. 88 percent say schools should teach sex education.

4. 77 percent say parents should have some influence in choosing the books that students read.

5. 62 percent believe that parents should be allowed to teach their children at home if they follow the required curriculum.

6. 55 percent say that schools place too much emphasis on sports.

7. 51 percent feel that television is a detriment to education; 35 percent see TV as an asset.

8. 46 percent support extending the school year to 11 or 12 months.

9. 35 percent say that parents who send their children to private or parochial schools should get a tax allowance.

10. Only 5 percent rate the U.S. education system as better than Japan's or Germany's.

11. 98 percent say that schools should teach students about drugs and their effects.

12. 67 percent say schools should teach "awareness and understanding" of different religions, while 57 percent support similar instruction about homosexuality.

13. Less than half (49 percent) give them high marks for teaching basic skills, and 60 percent say the schools do only a fair or poor job of encouraging creative thinking and curiosity.

14. More than half, however, rate as excellent or good the special programs for the gifted (57 percent) and special-needs children (52 percent), as well as the special classes such as art and gym (55 percent).

15. 52 percent say the quality of teaching is good, while 35 percent say it is fair.

16. One in two respondents (50 percent) says teachers' salaries are too low, 37 percent say they're just right, and 13 percent say they're too high.

17. 76 percent say more communication with parents would improve schools, while 75 percent indicated better quality teachers, 74 percent said a safer environment, 73 percent said more discipline, 67 percent said better qualified administrators, 63 percent said better drug education, 61 percent said smaller class size, 55 percent said better sex education, and 51 percent said a broader curriculum.

Adapted from Mark Clements, "What's Wrong with Our Schools?" *Parade Magazine*, May 16, 1993. These findings were based on a survey of 2,512 men and women, ages 18 to 75, and representative of the nation as a whole. Survey conducted in December 1992.

STAGE 2

Planning Technology Staff Development Programs

37

I Can Do Magic!

GOAL

▶ To convey to the group that technology staff development programs and experimentation with technology demands a creative mind-set.

FOCUS QUESTIONS

▶ Do technology programs demand a new mind-set?

▶ Why is it hard to come to terms with change and see things from a different perspective?

▶ Is creativity important when implementing technology-infused schools and technology-based learning?

STRATEGY

1. Tell the group: I can slide myself under this door. If there are any doubters, they are to come and stand on the other side of the door. When you close the door, write on a piece of paper the word *myself*.

2. Now slip the paper under the door.

3. Engage participants in discussion.

DISCUSSION QUESTIONS

▶ Are we thinking as creatively as we can when it comes to implementing and providing technology in our schools?

▶ Is technology going to demand that we think in more creative, abstract ways than we ever have before? If you think so, why?

What's Our Problem?

GOAL

▶ To enhance technology staff development teams' understanding of how to deal with and plan for important problems.

FOCUS QUESTIONS

▶ What are the problems that technology staff development teams will encounter?

▶ How can we plan efficiently and effectively to deal with problems?

STRATEGY

Share the following with participants.

1. The Pareto Principle states that "80 percent of the trouble comes from 20 percent of the problems." As a consequence, teams need to become accustomed to ranking problems that they are facing.

   The purpose is to identify which problems should be studied and then to identify which causes of the problems to address first.

   Teams should devise a strategy to focus their attention on the biggest problems. Most organizations and teams find that the most trouble comes from only a few problems.

2. To determine which problems are giving the team the greatest trouble:

   a. Divide the group into teams of four to six people.

   b. Next, direct teams to list specific examples that they are encountering with each problem.

   c. Based on the number of complaints or concerns related to each problem, allow teams to rank problems in order of importance.

   d. Allow teams to discuss the importance of these problems and to decide which ones need to be dealt with first, second, third, etc.

   e. Place that information on a chart and display it in all subsequent meetings, enabling teams to keep focusing on the most important problems.

DISCUSSION QUESTIONS

▶ What did you discover about the problems you are facing?

▶ Why is it important to rank the problems you are facing?

▶ Did the team activity reveal the Pareto Principle at work—"80 percent of the trouble comes from 20 percent of the problems?"

Seven Organizational Learning Disabilities

GOAL

▶ To illustrate that technology staff development program teams often suffer from organizational learning disabilities.

FOCUS QUESTION

▶ What are the seven organizational learning disabilities and how can we prevent them from minimizing the potential of the technology staff development program?

STRATEGY

1. Circulate the definitions of the seven organizational learning disabilities to participants (see next page).

2. Discuss definitions and illustrations of each of the seven disabilities.

3. Divide the group into teams to discuss whether the current program or any groups within the program have any of the seven learning disabilities. Discuss possible strategies for preventing or dealing with the disabilities.

4. Regroup participants and share strategies.

5. Develop a written plan that deals with the seven organizational learning disabilities.

DISCUSSION QUESTIONS

▶ Do we have agreement that the seven organizational learning disabilities are a problem or present potential problems?

▶ Is it difficult or easy to see evidence of the seven organization learning disabilities in our program?

▶ How are these disabilities preventing us from maximizing the potential of the emerging technologies to transform teaching and learning?

REFERENCE

Senge, P.M. (1990). *The Fifth Discipline—The Art & Practice of the Learning Organization.* New York: Doubleday. (Chapter 2).

Seven Organizational Learning Disabilities

1. I Am My Position
When people in organizations focus only on their position, they have little sense of responsibility for the results produced when all positions interact.

2. The Enemy Is Out There
Blaming someone or something outside ourselves when things go wrong. Assigning blame within and outside the organization.

3. The Illusion of Taking Charge
True proactiveness comes from seeing how we contribute to our own problems. All too often, proactiveness is reactiveness in disguise.

4. The Fixation on Events
Seeing only events. The primary threats to our survival, both of our organizations and of our societies, come not from sudden events but from slow, gradual processes.

5. The Parable of the Boiled Frog
Sensing threats to survival is geared to sudden changes in environment rather than slow, gradual change. Learning to see slow, gradual processes requires slowing down our frenetic pace and paying attention to the subtle, as well as the dramatic.

6. The Delusion of Learning from Experience
Organizations and people often experience a learning dilemma. A learning dilemma is believing that we learn from experience. However, in reality, we never directly experience the consequences of many of our most important decisions.

7. The Myth of Management Team
Maintaining the appearance of a cohesive team. Example: seeking to squelch disagreement to maintain appearance. Historical reasons: Schools never train us to admit that we do not know the answer, and most corporations reinforce that lesson by rewarding people who excel in advocating their views, not inquiring into complex issues.

Senge, P.M. (1990). *The Fifth Discipline—The Art & Practice of the Learning Organization*. New York: Doubleday. (Chapter 2).

You Are What You Write!

GOAL

▶ To orient technology team members about characteristics of effective technology guiding documents found in technology staff development programs.

FOCUS QUESTION

▶ Since goals, planning documents, technology mission statements, etc. are important documents in technology staff development programs, what standards should be set for judging their effectiveness?

STRATEGY

Begin this activity by using the following story:

1. In a recent edition of *The New York Times*, an article appeared which noted that the Lord's Prayer contains 56 words; the 23rd Psalm, 118 words; the Gettysburg Address, 226 words; and The Ten Commandments, 297 words, while the U.S. Department of Agriculture Directive on Pricing Cabbage weighed in at 15,629 words.

2. Since we don't want to follow in the path of the U.S. Department of Agriculture, what standards do we want to set for our technology-related guiding documents?

3. Brainstorm ideas. (Accept ideas such as "our documents must project a clear vision, clearly stated, stated in few, clear terms," etc.)

4. Now get the group to make decisions about the nature of the technology guiding documents.

5. Remind the group of the following: People are bombarded by hundreds, even thousands, of communications each day. When other stakeholders read about our technology staff development program, our materials and messages must have (a) relevance, (b) clarity, and (c) dramatic impact. **Remember, just like people are what they eat, you are what you write!**

DISCUSSION QUESTIONS

▶ Now that we have brainstormed characteristics of technology staff development guiding documents, how can we ensure that we will adhere to these guidelines?

▶ On what basis will other stakeholders judge us by our written technology staff development program materials?

Technology Planning: Scenario Planning

GOAL

▶ To provide alternative ways of looking at planning by using scenarios.

FOCUS QUESTION

▶ How can we plan technology in the classroom without getting bogged down with traditional planning tools of goals and objectives?

STRATEGY

Relate the following:

1. Begin by defining technology planning scenarios. Technology planning scenarios are written documents which allow teachers to describe how they want to use and explore the emerging technologies in their classroom. Rather than engaging in traditional planning activities such as goal and objective identification, the teacher or team prepares a narrative or essay. Specifically, the narrative tells (a) what the students will be doing, (b) what the teacher will be doing, (c) what emerging technologies will be used (resources), and (d) what products will be produced with the emerging technologies.

2. Now assign the following: Write a scenario that describes how you want to use technology in your classroom next year.

3. You may want to provide examples or excerpts from previously written scenarios.

DISCUSSION QUESTIONS

▶ How did you feel when writing technology scenarios as compared to writing plans in a traditional form of goals, objectives, lesson plans, etc.?

▶ Do you prefer planning in a traditional manner or a more creative manner?

▶ What are the advantages and disadvantages of scenario planning as a tool for integrating technology into teaching and learning?

TECHNOLOGY PLANNING: SCENARIO PLANNING—EXAMPLE

A typical student who is working in my classroom:

Peter Rabbit. A six-year-old whose first language is not English is reading *The Tale of Peter Rabbit* on a computer in my classroom. He reads some aloud; he has the computer read some to him; he investigates the pictures by clicking on their various elements. The text is in English, but if he clicks twice on a word he can hear it in Spanish. I come by and discuss the story with him, and suggest he write a story of his own. He pulls up a talking children's word processor on the same computer and begins to compose, hearing what he writes. Later that evening, we see him at home, where his mother asks him what he wants for a bedtime story. The child pulls a floppy disk from his pocket and says he would like to read the story that he wrote today in school.

Looking Forward to Plan Backwards

GOALS

► To facilitate participants thinking about what accomplishments they want to achieve over the next few decades.

► To allow participants to create a vision of their program by looking far into the future—imaging the future which allows us to plan forward.

FOCUS QUESTION

► Why is it important to be able to see the "big picture" when engaging in technology planning?

STRATEGY

Relate the following:

1. It is important that we have an idea of what we want to accomplish in our technology staff development program. Rather than develop conventional strategies of planning, I want you to do the following:

   a. Close your eyes and imagine that you and your friends are gathered for a celebration in honor of the many accomplishments and achievements in your technology staff development program. There are several speakers who are telling stories of the accomplishments relating to the origin and growth of the program.

   b. Imagine that you are listening to the speaker. On a piece of paper, write down the specific accomplishments of the group that are being mentioned by the speaker.

   c. On the other side of the paper, write down what the other speakers are saying about **you and your contributions** to the program.

   d. Instruct the participants to break up into small groups (four to six).

   e. Now have participants read and share their ideas.

   f. Use this new information to form the planning ideas of your technology staff development program.

DISCUSSION QUESTIONS

► How can we use ideas about the future to build a vision today?

► What individual accomplishments were identified and how can we facilitate these achievements?

► Why is it important that we revisit this "planning backward activity" periodically?

► Why is it critically important to look at this vision from a "present-to-future" and "future-to-present" perspective?

Looking for the Right Answer

GOAL

▶ To illustrate that a mind-set of "there is only one right answer" hinders and kills creativity.

FOCUS QUESTION

▶ Why is looking for more than one right answer important when working with technology-based learning?

STRATEGY

1. Draw the following dot on the board or flip-chart:

2. Then ask the following question: "What is it?"

3. If someone says "a dot," put that answer on the board/flip-chart, and stop.

4. Now, write the following answers in the right hand column: (1) cigar butt, (2) top of telephone pole, (3) star, (4) pebble, and (5) squashed bug. As you are writing these answers on the board, tell the group that these are typical answers from kindergarten students.

5. What do the two lists illustrate?

DISCUSSION QUESTIONS

▶ Why do adults typically look for the right answer and not look for several correct answers?

▶ What happens to children's creativity over the years?

▶ How does working with technology enhance a learner's creativity?

▶ Do teachers overlook the inherent potential of technology to stimulate student creativity? Why?

REFERENCE

Adapted from von Oech, R. (1986). *A Kick in the Seat of the Pants*. New York: HarperCollins.

Are You an Entrepreneur?

GOAL

▶ To illustrate how other pioneers overcame great odds because they had a vision and believed in what they were doing.

FOCUS QUESTIONS

▶ What makes some pioneers successful?

▶ What can we learn from pioneers who had similar problems such as limited resources?

STRATEGY

1. Tell or show the following information:

   In the 1970s, a young man of 16 walked out of a computer store with an order for 50 computers worth $25,000. But no bank would advance him the capital to build the things. Finally, a distributor advanced him $20,000 worth of parts for 30 days.

   The young man and his partner started an assembly line on a dining table, until the boy's mother objected. They wound up in a garage. The boy's sister put together boards for $1 each while she watched TV. His mother took phone messages and served coffee to visiting salesmen. Then, finally, this fledgling company wrote a business plan and wangled its first investor.

2. Allow the group to guess the identity of these persons. If no one answers correctly, explain that this boy was Steven Jobs and his partner was Steve Wozniak. The fledgling company was Apple Computer.

3. Allow the group to brainstorm what relevance this story has to technology leaders and teachers who struggle to find resources for purchasing technology resources.

DISCUSSION QUESTIONS

▶ What is the lesson to be learned from the story?

▶ How are educators (early adopters of the emerging technologies) similar to Jobs and Wozniak? Dissimilar?

The Most Successful Ad in History

GOAL
▶ To illustrate how other pioneers rose to greatness—just like the people involved in the emerging technologies are pioneers.

FOCUS QUESTION
▶ What is expected of us as pioneers in transforming education with the emerging technologies?

STRATEGY

1. Provide the following information in a visual manner.

> *"Men wanted for hazardous journey. Low wages, bitter cold, long hours of complete darkness. Safe return doubtful. Honour and recognition in the event of success."*
>
> E. Shackleton (1907)

2. Let participants study the ad for a few seconds. Then provide the following explanation:

   "Early in this century, this classified ad appeared in *The Times* of London.

   Ernest Shackleton was looking for a hardy crew he could take on his quest to discover the South Pole. The next morning, over 5,000 men were waiting outside *The Times'* offices. Shackleton reached the Pole in 1907."

3. Allow the group to brainstorm what relevance this type of ad has to pioneers who are exploring the emerging technologies.

4. Ask the group to write their own ad which could be used to recruit faculty and other stakeholders who want to use emerging technologies as tools for transforming education.

DISCUSSION QUESTIONS
▶ What is the lesson to be learned from Shackleton's ad?
▶ How are early adopters of the emerging technologies similar to Shackleton and his recruits? Dissimilar?
▶ What will our rewards be for success? Failure?

REFERENCE
Adapted from Anderson, D.M. (1993). The most successful ad in history. *Success, 40*, (1).

Focus on Your Strengths

GOAL

▶ To allow participants to recognize how they can be successful with emerging technologies by learning how to focus on their strengths.

FOCUS QUESTION

▶ Why is it important for us to focus on our strengths and not our weaknesses?

STRATEGY

Relate the following:

1. The highest levels of achievement come when people are matched with activities that use their strengths. Sounds like common sense? Hardly! It is rarely applied, according to Gallup consultants Donald Clifton and Paula Nelson. Instead of spending time trying to correct your weaknesses—as many of us are taught to do—Clifton and Nelson recommend that you should focus on your special talents.

2. Relate the following tips:

   l. **Pick one strength to pursue.** Raw intelligence does not guarantee success. Rather, what distinguishes spectacular achievers from low achievers is that the former are focused on what they want to do in life.

   2. **Exercise your strength daily.** Ultimate excellence is a product of total commitment, hard work over the long-term, and heeding the message, "If it doesn't feel good, you're not practicing a strength."

   3. **Ignore weaknesses that don't hinder you.** Work on a problem only if it's lessening your productivity or self-esteem. By managing your weaknesses, you allow your strengths to overpower them, ultimately making them irrelevant.

   4. **Look for complementary partners.** Some strengths only reveal themselves when combined with those of other people. Examples include the Wright Brothers, Rodgers and Hammerstein, and Fred Astaire and Ginger Rogers.

   5. **Develop a support system.** Everyone needs support of some sort. Find others who can do the things you don't do well. Don't tackle chores that you don't do well. Control your weaknesses through a support system.

DISCUSSION QUESTIONS

▶ What are your strengths as they relate to using the emerging technologies? What are your weaknesses? How will you deal with your strengths and weaknesses?

▶ Why is it a waste of time and energy to try to fix all of our weaknesses?

▶ What people do you know or individuals from history can you identify that characterize the use of these five elements of success?

REFERENCE

Adapted from Clifton, D.O. & Nelson, P. (1992). *Soar with Your Strengths.* New York: Delacorte Press.

48

Worrying Makes You Less Effective!

GOALS
- ▶ To illustrate how worrying can be a drag on creative energy.
- ▶ To suggest different ways of thinking about problems.

FOCUS QUESTIONS
- ▶ What problems are worth worrying about?
- ▶ How can you resolve problems (worries) that confront you?

STRATEGY

1. Ask participants to brainstorm what they worry about (as it relates to using and promoting the emerging technologies as tools for school transformation). List these worries on the board/flip chart.

2. Then allow participants to prioritize (order of importance from greatest to least) these worries.

3. Relate the following information: Psychologist Wolf J. Rinke believes that "one of the worst drags on your energy is worrying. Not all worries are useless, but only 8 percent are 'legitimate'—that is, under your control such that you can do something about them. The other 92 percent are 'worthless worries.'" Rinke's suggests eight steps:
   1. Clarify what it is that your are worried about. Write it down.
   2. Ask yourself if there is anything you can do to affect the situation. If not, it's a worthless worry—skip to #8. If there is, go to #3.
   3. Identify the worst possible outcome.
   4. Ask yourself if you can live with the worst possible outcome. If so, go to #6. If not, go to #5.
   5. Do everything in your power to solve the problem right now.
   6. Make an action plan that will solve the problem entirely or minimize its bad consequences.
   7. Take action.
   8. Quit worrying. Either it's too late, or worrying won't make a difference.

4. Brainstorm ideas about how to put Rinke's eight steps into practice.

DISCUSSION QUESTIONS
- ▶ How can this process of dealing with worrying help technology leaders as they plan and implement technology staff development programs?

REFERENCE
Rinke, W. (1992). *Make It a Winning Life: Success Strategies for Life, Love, and Business*. Rockville, MD: Achievement Publishers.

Hiring a Consultant

GOAL

▶ To create an awareness about the importance of hiring a consultant for technology staff development programs.

FOCUS QUESTION

▶ What things should be considered when hiring a consultant?

STRATEGY

1. Stress the following point: Hiring a consultant may be one of the most important decisions made in a technology staff development program.

2. Allow participants to brainstorm about the role of consultants in any technology staff development program.

3. Get participants to develop a leadership profile of an excellent consultant.

4. Share information entitled, "Hiring a Consultant: 10 Tips" (see next page).

DISCUSSION QUESTIONS

▶ How should you select a consultant?
▶ On what basis should you make a selection?
▶ What qualities should you look for in a consultant?

Hiring a Consultant: 10 Tips

1. **Define your needs.**
   Look for your consultant after you have determined your needs. Don't find a consultant who tells you what you need.

2. **Contact other schools.**
   Find out who else has used this consultant. Call more than one school. Talk to people with firsthand knowledge of the consultant's abilities.

3. **Talk to vendors who know consultants.**
   Vendors have a wealth of information about consultants. Don't be afraid to bounce their opinion off of formal recommendations from other sources.

4. **Contact a variety of consultants.**
   Interviewing a variety of consultants is time-consuming but sometimes necessary to find the best deal.

5. **Send your needs to the potential consultants and ask for recommendations.**
   Get consultants to tailor their program and materials to your needs. Otherwise, consultants will use what has worked for them before in other schools.

6. **Find out how the consultant works with people.**
   One of the most important attributes of consultants is their human-relations skills. Do they get along with others? Are they flexible? Do they work well with a wide range of personalities?

7. **Draw up a written contract.**
   It is almost always a good idea to work from a contract. Spell out the conditions so that both parties know what is expected.

8. **Develop a rapport with consultants when you hire them.**
   You get the best results from consultants when they have a personal investment in your school and in you as a person. People will go the extra mile if you personalize the relationship.

9. **Evaluate the performance of the consultant in a variety of ways.**
   Solicit feedback from a wide range of people. Get it in writing and orally. Share it with the consultant so that he or she knows what went right and how to better serve you next time.

10. **Don't expect the consultant to do everything for you.**
    Consultants can only do so much. Never expect miracles, but demand accountability. Ask yourself if the consultant delivered what you expected.

Where Should We Focus Our Training?

GOAL

▶ To illustrate the importance of targeting basic skills which should be taught in the technology staff development program.

FOCUS QUESTIONS

▶ What skills do faculty need in the area of the emerging technologies?

▶ Why is it important to pinpoint skill areas in technology staff development programs?

STRATEGY

1. Ask the group to brainstorm possible competencies that they wish to possess in the emerging technologies.

2. Circulate the definitions (see next page) concerning six basic technology skill areas.

3. Engage participants in a discussion concerning the importance and priority of each skill in any technology staff development program.

DISCUSSION QUESTIONS

▶ Which technology skills should be dealt with in the program?

▶ Which technology skills should be dealt with first, second, third, etc. in the program?

▶ What happens to technology staff development programs that do not have a plan for teaching technology skills?

□□□

Six Basic Technology Skills in Technology Staff Development Programs

1. **Computer Operation and Word Processing**—skills related to turning computer on and off, printing, routine procedures of computer navigation, etc., as well as the art of entering text and manipulating text-based documents. This competency can be described in terms of a user's ability to "crunch words."

2. **Emerging Technologies**—skills (in addition to the computer) which involve the operation of interactive videodisc player, modem, videotape recorder, television, fax, CD-ROM (compact disc-read only memory), satellite, LCD (liquid crystal display) Panel, etc. This competency can be described in terms of a user's ability to "navigate electronically."

3. **Spreadsheet Construction**—skills related to organization of numerical information into ledgerlike electronic forms for analysis and calculations. This competency can be described in terms of the user's ability to "crunch numbers."

4. **Database Construction**—skills related to the construction of an aggregation of data together with a collection of operations that facilitates searching, sorting, and recombining activities. This competency can be described in terms of a user's ability to "crunch data."

5. **Networking**—skills related to communication with others on a computer network, and connection of teachers to major databases inside and outside the school. This competency can be described in terms of a user's ability to "communicate electronically over distance and time."

6. **Visual-audio Data Processing**—skills related to using sound, video, graphics, text, etc. in any application that are shared in common (i.e., HyperCard™, LinkWay Live™, etc.). This competency can be described in terms of a user's ability to "crunch pictures, sound, and text."

Implementing Technology Staff Development Programs

How Important Is Group Cooperation?

GOAL

▶ To show the importance of cooperation which contributes to group efficiency and survival.

FOCUS QUESTIONS

▶ Why is it important for people to cooperate in small groups or teams?

▶ What cooperative behaviors can we learn from the animal and insect world?

STRATEGY

1. Divide the group into smaller groups of three to eight.

2. Assign roles of either Geese or Bees.

3. Let the group engage in play (e.g., act like a group of bees or geese for only a few seconds or minutes).

4. Now set the stage for the groups to engage in brainstorming about problems and necessary cooperative behavior which are linked to their survival by asking the following questions:

Bees

Problem: Your colony is undergoing brutally sub-zero weather this winter. Your colony will not survive unless you cooperate.

Question: What strategies will you employ to survive?

Geese

Problem: Your flock is preparing to fly hundreds of miles during seasonal migration. However, food and water is limited.

Question: What will you do to cooperate so that you maximize your efficiency and effectiveness?

5. Allow the group to brainstorm several minutes to arrive at possible answers.

6. If no group comes up with appropriate answers, provide answers to promote additional discussion (see next page).

DISCUSSION QUESTIONS

▶ If birds and insects have had to learn cooperative behaviors, why is it important for people to learn how to cooperate?

▶ Are there strategies which we could use that would allow us to become as efficient as the insect world and bird world? What would they be?

How Important Is Group Cooperation?

WHY DO GEESE FLY IN "V" FORMATION?

Engineers have found that each bird, by flapping its wings, creates an uplift for the bird that follows. Together, the whole flock gains something like 70 percent greater flying range than if they were journeying alone.

HOW DO BEES SURVIVE THE WINTER?

Bees live through the winter by mutual aid. They form into a ball and keep up a dance. Then they change places; those that have been out move to the center, and those at the center move out. Thus, they survive the winter.

If those at the center insisted on staying there, keeping the others at the edges, they would all perish.

ARE ALL BEES THE SAME?

It appears that all bees are not the same. For years, fruit growers have relied on honeybees for the basic task of carrying pollen from blossom to blossom.

But farmers are impressed with the work habits of another insect: the bumblebee.

These burlier, hairy bees work longer hours than honeybees, and they don't mind toiling in the rain or cold weather.

That's why farmers are interested to see whether bumblebees can be used for pollination in other crops. Can insects and humans learn to work together?

Learning in Teams Who Use Technology

GOAL
▶ To orient participants about the difference between dependent learning and interdependent learning.

FOCUS QUESTIONS
▶ What behaviors are expected of people who work in teams?

▶ How do these new behaviors contrast with previous behaviors which have been prevalent in group work of the past?

STRATEGY
Adjustment to team learning can require a considerable shift—especially if people have had only limited experiences in learning teams. Articulating expectations can be quite important for helping people make the adjustment.

1. Divide participants into groups of four to six.

2. Share the document entitled "Shifting to Team Learning—Continuum" (see next page).

3. Have participants discuss where they are on the continuum (for each item).

4. Have participants generate additional items which would reflect a major shift from teacher-centered learning to student-centered learning.

DISCUSSION QUESTIONS
▶ Why is team learning so important to the study of the emerging technologies?

▶ Why do some people find it difficult to shift from dependent learning (teacher-centered) to interdependent learning (team-centered)?

▶ Do we have any evidence that the world of work is shifting from independent or dependent learning (trainer-centered) to team-centered learning?

Shifting to Team Learning— Continuum

⟵————————————————⟶

OLD BEHAVIORS	NEW BEHAVIORS
1. playing it safe	1. high risk-aking
2. blocker	2. facilitator of others
3. seeing obstacles	3. seeing opportunities
4. getting your ticket punched	4. leadership growth
5. individual focus	5. team focus
6. intolerance	6. tolerance
7. old paradigm	7. new paradigm
8. content interest	8. learning to learn
9. dependent or independent	9. interdependent
10. change as enemy	10. change as friend
11. no tech	11. tech as empowerment tool
12. schools as we've known them	12. school transformation
13. manager	13. learning leader
14. teacher as knowledge giver	14. teacher as facilitator/coach
15. isolated events	15. systems perspective
16. past orientation	16. future orientation
17. talking the talk	17. walking the walk (modeling)
18. segmented learning	18. integrated learning
19. closed	19. open
20. finding reasons to explain failure	20. using failure to learn

Teams

GOAL

▶ To explore the meaning of teams and team work in technology staff development programs.

FOCUS QUESTIONS

▶ What are teams?

▶ What is the purpose of teams in technology staff development programs?

STRATEGY

Review and circulate "Team-Learning Axioms" (see next page).

1. Allow participants to discuss the meaning of team learning in technology staff development programs. Specifically, address these two questions:

   a. What are the different roles in team learning?

   b. What is the relationship between leaders and team members in technology-related staff development programs?

2. Direct participants to come up with their own axioms which reflect their beliefs about team learning.

3. Allow participants to synthesize these axioms into a profile of team leadership.

4. Remind teams to revisit these axioms regularly when they have successes and failures.

DISCUSSION QUESTIONS

▶ How do the axioms impact your perception of teams and team learning?

▶ Of what value are axioms to technology-based learning teams?

▶ What basic axioms of teams and team learning should be most highlighted in your technology staff development program?

▶ Are all of the axioms reflective of your concept of team learning? Which ones are? Are not?

Team-Learning Axioms

▶ A team meeting is a place where everybody talks, nobody listens, and everyone disagrees afterward.

▶ A team is four to six people trying to park one car.

▶ Most people are willing to meet other team members halfway. The problem is that most team members are poor judges of distance.

▶ The greatest need of teams is to find a key to unlock gridlock.

▶ Team cooperation and collaboration is spelled with two letters—WE!

▶ The team is the symphony, the team leader is the conductor.

▶ Teams do not work where teams are divided.

▶ We must share the vision to be in harmony with change.

▶ A small river will carry a lot of water if it keeps running.

▶ Coming together is a beginning; keeping together is progress; working together is success.

▶ We all hang together or we hang separately.

▶ We didn't all come over in the same ship, but we're all in the same boat.

▶ The river is powerful because many drops of water have learned the secret of cooperation.

▶ Effective teams build bridges—not walls.

▶ Effective teams learn how to be agreeable when they disagree.

▶ As spokes get nearer to the hub of the wheel, they become closer together.

▶ Team harmony is seldom achieved without personal sacrifice.

▶ Cooperation is doing with a smile what you had to do anyway.

▶ You have a right to your opinion as long as it agrees with mine.

▶ It takes two to make up after a quarrel.

Pick a Color!

GOAL

▶ To promote team-building characteristics.

FOCUS QUESTION

▶ How can we learn to cooperate better in technology-based learning teams?

STRATEGY

1. Break the group up into teams.

2. Have participants select a color that reflects who they are! Then provide the following directions:

   a. Pick a color that you like. It can be a color in your mind's eye, one that you're wearing, or one you see in the room.

   b. Don't worry if everyone in the room picks the same color. You'll all see the color differently.

   c. Take turns speaking. Each of you should take up to one minute. Some of you may be done in 15 to 20 seconds.

   d. Speak in the first person (e.g., "I am blue because. . .," "I am yellow because . . .").

   e. You can be funny or serious.

3. Allow groups to debrief by discussing what they experienced when they selected colors.

DISCUSSION QUESTIONS

▶ What did you learn from this activity?
▶ How can we apply what you learned to our technology-based learning teams?

Praise Behind Your Back

GOAL
▶ To promote team-building characteristics.

FOCUS QUESTION
▶ How can we learn to cooperate better when working in technology-based learning teams?

STRATEGY

1. Divide participants into groups.

2. Tell them you are going to play a game called "Praise behind your back!"

3. Provide the following directions:

   a. Have one person turn his or her back, so he or she can't see the others, but can hear them. (This person is in the "hot seat." This person should have a pen and pencil ready to take notes).

   b. For about two or three minutes, the group should talk to each other **(about the hot-seat person's good qualities).** The hot-seat person should take notes.

   c. After you're finished talking about that person, go to the next team member until everyone has heard him- or herself described.

   ### KEY RULES FOR TEAM MEMBERS:
   ▶ Describe assets or positive qualities only. *Nothing negative.*
   ▶ Be specific in your praise. Do not talk in general terms.

   ### KEY RULES FOR HOT-SEAT PERSON:
   ▶ Write everything down. Write legibly.
   ▶ Don't respond to what you hear.
   ▶ Use sign language to other team members if you can't hear clearly.
   ▶ When everyone is finished, you simply turn around. Make no comment about what was said.

4. Allow participants to discuss their experience.

DISCUSSION QUESTIONS
▶ How did you feel about the comments?
▶ What did you learn from this activity?
▶ How can we apply what you learned to your technology-based learning team?

Why Do Some Team Members Excel?

GOAL

▶ To get team members to identify what skills make an average team member become an excellent team member.

FOCUS QUESTION

▶ What skills or qualities do I need to become a excellent team player?

STRATEGY

1. Divide the group into teams of four to six.

2. Orient them to the need to focus on effective team membership.

3. Allow participants to brainstorm effective team-member qualities.

4. Then circulate the audit (see next page).

5. Allow groups to discuss their audit score.

DISCUSSION QUESTIONS

1. What does it take to be an excellent team player?

2. What specific differences are there in excellent team players and average team players?

Why Do Some Team Members Excel?

TRUE OR FALSE:

_____ **1.** I have learned self-discipline. I can persevere when others give up, and I have the capacity to postpone, but not forgo, gratification.

_____ **2.** I bring out the best in people. I evoke affection and loyalty from people. I seek out people that I can learn from, then I try to bring people together to learn from one another.

_____ **3.** I try to develop special skills to become successful. I recognize that success leads to other successes, and I help the team work toward these successes.

_____ **4.** I keep promises when I can. I believe that keeping your word is important and that I can be counted on by other team members.

_____ **5.** I try to bounce back from defeat and help others deal with defeat positively.

SCORING—Ideally, you marked all items "True." Here's how to score your responses:

      5 — Excellent
      4 — Above Average
      3 — Average
      2 — Below Average
  1 or 0 — Poor

The Human Chain

GOAL

▶ To demonstrate the critical importance of teamwork.

FOCUS QUESTION

▶ Why is it important to learn to work together?

STRATEGY

1. Divide the group into teams of six or eight.

2. Instruct each team to form a circle.

3. Provide the following directions:

   Extend your left hand across the circle and grasp the left hand of the member who is opposite you. Then extend your right hand across the circle and grasp the right hand of another individual.

4. Your goal is to untangle the human chain of interlocking arms without letting go of anyone's hands.

5. Options:
   a. Put a time limit on the activity.
   b. Provide a prize for the team that accomplishes the task in the least amount of time.

6. In groups or all together focus on discussion questions.

DISCUSSION QUESTIONS

▶ What lessons can be learned from the human chain?
▶ Why is it important that people learn to cooperate?
▶ What individual behaviors contributed or hindered each team's efforts?
▶ What team skills are important to the success of the group?

Technology Is Poetry to My Ears

GOAL

▶ To show participants that using the talents of all team members produces a better, more creative product in the end.

FOCUS QUESTIONS

▶ Is it important to have all team members involved when engaging in technology implementation?

▶ Does involving more participants increase the credibility of the technology staff development program? Why or why not?

STRATEGY

1. On a blank piece of paper, have one person begin by writing one line of poetry. The paper is folded over to hide the one line and is passed to the right. When passed, the only thing you tell the person is the last word you used, so that the next person can think of something that rhymes or doesn't, as the case may be. Then the paper is folded over again.

2. The paper is passed around until everyone has made a contribution to the poem. Then each person or a selected group of people read their completed poem to the group.

DISCUSSION QUESTIONS

▶ Is it important for all team members to be involved in such a way that their contribution can be clearly seen?

▶ Do too many contributions by team members make things too complex and confusing?

Consensus Building

GOAL

▶ To illustrate that technology-based learning teams need to understand consensus— both what it is and what it is not.

FOCUS QUESTION

▶ What is the importance of consensus building?

STRATEGY

1. Circulate the "Consensus Building Audit" for technology teams (see next page).

2. Then have participants score the audit. Scoring: All ten items are true.

3. Discuss audit scores and examples of consensus building.

4. Divide the group into small teams to discuss if the current technology staff development program or any groups within the technology staff development program can benefit from training in consensus building.

5. Regroup participants and share strategies.

DISCUSSION QUESTIONS

▶ How important is consensus when making team decisions?

▶ How can technology staff development team members be trained in consensus building?

Consensus Building Audit

___T ___F **1.** Consensus building **is** when a group's goal is to reach decisions that best reflect the thinking of all group members.

___T ___F **2.** Consensus **is** finding a proposal acceptable enough that all members can support it; no member opposes it.

___T ___F **3.** Consensus **is not** a unanimous vote (consensus may not represent everyone's first priority).

___T ___F **4.** Consensus **is not** a majority vote. In a majority vote, only the majority gets something they are happy with. People in the minority may get something they don't want at all, which is not what consensus is all about.

___T ___F **5.** Consensus **is not** having everyone totally satisfied.

___T ___F **6.** Consensus **requires** time.

___T ___F **7.** Consensus **requires** active participation of all group members.

___T ___F **8.** Consensus **requires** skill in communication: listening, conflict resolution, and discussion-facilitation abilities.

___T ___F **9.** Consensus **requires** creative thinking and open-mindedness.

___T ___F **10.** You have **achieved consensus** when everyone can live with the decision even though not everyone may be satisfied with the decision.

Your School Has Just Been Given $100,000!

GOAL

▶ To highlight the importance of establishing priorities when making technology purchases.

FOCUS QUESTIONS

▶ What technology purchases must be made first?

▶ On what basis do we make these decisions?

STRATEGY

1. Divide the group into teams of three to five, and provide the following role-playing directions:

   a. Assume that your school (not school district) has just been given $100,000 to invest in the emerging technologies.

   b. Assume the following stipulation has been placed on the use of the money by the benefactor. *The money must be used to help students become prepared for the 21st century.*

   c. Assume that **no** school district policy exists which provides you direction **or** assume that a school policy exists which indicates that the site-council must provide advice and counsel to the school in these situations.

   d. Your challenge: What should be done with the money? What are your group's priorities?

2. Now discuss findings from small groups and achieve consensus in a large-group setting.

DISCUSSION QUESTIONS

▶ What does this tell us about the value of small-group and large-group effort and consensus building?

▶ What are the key skills of effective consensus building?

▶ What does this tell us about the value of establishing priorities in technology staff development programs?

▶ On what basis (i.e., criteria) did you make your decisions?

Solving Conflict with Win-Win Thinking

GOAL

▶ To facilitate participants' understanding and empathy of win-win situations.

FOCUS QUESTION

▶ Why is it important to be empathic about solving problems and adopting a win-win mentality rather than a win-lose outlook?

STRATEGY

1. Instruct the group to divide into pairs.

2. Ask participants to sit down across from each other.

3. Designate one person as Handwrestler A and the other as Handwrestler B.

4. Partners should clasp hands: right with right or left with left, depending on their preference. Remind them to keep their elbows on the table.

5. Ask them to wrestle with firm pressure.

6. Let participants arm wrestle for a few moments without hurting each other.

7. Then tell them to stop resisting on alternate attempts—Handwrestler A forfeits one, Handwrestler B the next. Allow for approximately 10 or 20 attempts.

8. Then share the following:

   "Everyone can be a winner in life. We can have situations where both parties win. In developing innovative programs with technology, we need to work in a manner where everyone can feel like a winner and not feel that unwarranted competition dictates a win-lose situation among cooperating participants."

DISCUSSION QUESTIONS

▶ How can we use win-win ideas in our technology staff development program?

▶ How did it feel when both you and your partner won?

▶ What negative effect can win-lose thinking have on faculty in technology staff development programs?

Adapted from Covey, S. (1989). *Seven Habits of Highly Effective People*. New York: Firestone.

Seven Principles of Breakthrough Thinking

GOAL

▶ To illustrate that technology staff development program leaders and technology-based learning teams need to learn how to problem-solve.

FOCUS QUESTION

▶ What are the seven principles of breakthrough thinking and how can they be used to maximize the potential of technology staff development programs?

STRATEGY

1. Circulate the definitions of the seven principles of breakthrough thinking (see next page).

2. Discuss definitions and illustrations of each of the seven principles.

3. Divide the group into teams to discuss how they could use breakthrough thinking.

4. Regroup participants and share ideas.

5. Develop a written plan that deals with using breakthrough thinking as a holistic approach to problem solving.

DISCUSSION QUESTIONS

▶ Are we in agreement that the seven principles of breakthrough thinking are important? Why or why not?

▶ How could mastery of these seven principles maximize the potential of the emerging technologies to transform teaching and learning?

REFERENCE

Nadler, G. & Hibino, S. (1990). *Breakthrough Thinking—Why We Must Change the Way We Solve Problems, and the Seven Principles to Achieve This*. Rocklin, CA: Prima Publishing.

Seven Principles of Breakthrough Thinking (Problem Solving)

1. UNIQUENESS PRINCIPLE

Whatever the apparent similarities, each problem is unique and requires an approach that dwells on its own contextual needs.

2. THE PURPOSES PRINCIPLE

Focusing on purposes helps strip away nonessential aspects to avoid working on the wrong problem.

3. THE SOLUTION-AFTER-NEXT PRINCIPLE

Innovation can be stimulated and solutions made more effective by working backward from an ideal target solution.

4. THE SYSTEMS PRINCIPLE

Every problem is part of a larger system. Understanding the elements and dimensions of a system matrix lets you determine in advance the complexities you must incorporate in the implementation of the solution.

5. THE LIMITED INFORMATION COLLECTION PRINCIPLE

Knowing too much about a problem initially can prevent you from seeing some excellent alternative solutions.

6. THE PEOPLE DESIGN PRINCIPLE

The people who will carry out and use a solution must work together in developing the solution with Breakthrough Thinking. The proposed solution should include only the minimal, critical details, so that the users of the solution can have some flexibility in applying it.

7. THE BETTERMENT TIME-LINE PRINCIPLE

A sequence of purpose-directed solutions is a bridge to a better future. Incremental improvement by making small changes is important to long-term growth.

Adapted from Nadler, G. & Hibino, S. (1990). *Breakthrough Thinking—Why We Must Change the Way We Solve Problems, and the Seven Principles to Achieve This*. Rocklin, CA: Prima Publishing.

Ouch! That E-Mail Hurts!

GOAL

▶ To explore strategies for mending bruised relationships in technology staff development teams.

FOCUS QUESTIONS

▶ How should people deal with hurt feelings?

▶ Why do people find it difficult to say that they are sorry?

STRATEGY

1. Share the following story:

One day Larry was very frustrated with the demands that team members had been placing on him with the assignments. Teams members wanted Larry to do his fair share but he had many other demands—his wife was sick and the in-laws were staying at his house.

My team leader is a slave driver, he thought. How can he be so demanding and bossy?

He typed a message on his computer terminal to an understanding colleague. Then he sent the note over e-mail to his friend's computer—at least, he meant to.

The next day, Larry realized his mistake when he saw the look of profound hurt on the team leader's face! His whole team got his e-mail message. What a screwup! The damage was done! How can Larry get out of this fix?

2. Share the five strategies identified in "Dealing with Hurt Feelings" (see next page).

3. Get participants to identify their own strategies (group rules) for dealing with hurt feelings and misunderstandings.

DISCUSSION QUESTIONS

▶ Why do we find it hard to make amends for hurt we have caused?

▶ What is the best way to apologize and make things right when we have hurt someone?

Dealing with Hurt Feelings

1. TALK IT OUT TO WORK IT OUT!

Most people say they are sorry and turn and hide. But by talking with the person, fences can be mended. In Larry's case, he should have asked to talk to the team leader in private. The solution is to focus on how to handle the situation maturely rather than just reacting emotionally.

2. SHOW YOUR TRUE FEELINGS.

The embarrassment that comes from public error often tempts people to be overly reserved in their apologies. The victim is more calm when you show concern or remorse. Most people are quite understanding if you admit you are at fault.

Larry's team leader will be very forgiving if honesty and forthrightness prevails.

3. MAKE IT RIGHT WITH THE PERSON YOU OFFENDED.

After the apologies and excuses, you must act to reverse the damage. In Larry's case, the apology and conference with the team leader was the act of restitution. In many cases, you need to come up with a new system that will prevent the same mistake and solve other problems at the same time—that is the way to restore people's faith and confidence!

4. FORGIVE YOURSELF AFTER MAKING RESTITUTION.

Some people have difficulty forgiving themselves even when it was just circumstances or fate. Sometimes mistakes are fate—being the right person at the wrong time. If you are limited or have no control of the incident, forgive yourself. Learn to let go what you can't control.

5. LEARN FROM YOUR MISTAKE.

If your bad habits get you in trouble, you need to change the way you do things. Correct the behavior which causes the problem. See foul-ups as opportunities for self-improvement.

Six Steps for Handling Disagreements

GOAL

▶ To show that technology leaders need to see other people's objections to their ideas as opportunities to improve their own ideas.

FOCUS QUESTION

▶ How do you react when someone disagrees with you?

STRATEGY

1. Break the group into two teams and role-play the following situation:

Group #1: One of the team members objects to the way that the school is using existing resources for purchasing new hardware and software.

Specifically, one of the technology staff development committee members tells you that the money expenditures for hardware are too great and that there is not enough evidence (research) to support large expenditures of money. Respond to the objection. Have Group #2 observe the role-playing.

Group #2: Role-play the same situation again, but have the group leader adopt the following steps when objections surface. Have Group #1 observe the role-playing.

1. Stay Positive—Most objections are really just hard questions. Remain patient, self-controlled, interested, and confident. Sit tall and hold your arms open; face the person.

3. Ask—Enlist the other person's help by getting him or her to clarify his or her concerns.

4. Listen—Discipline yourself to hear with a "third ear." Listen for words that need more definition, and ask more and better questions.

5. Respond—Resolve the objection, drawing on all your knowledge of that person and his or her perspective.

6. Check—Once you've responded to the objection through reconciliation, gauge if the person is satisfied. Get him or her to respond—silence does not mean agreement.

2. Bring participants together and have the two groups discuss their experiences and observations.

DISCUSSION QUESTIONS

▶ Compare the leader's response in the two role-playing situations. Was there a difference when you used positive leadership skills? Why or why not?
▶ How difficult is it to adopt the six steps of positive leadership? Why?

Zingers

GOAL

▶ To get participants to recognize the importance of group cooperation in technology staff development programs.

FOCUS QUESTIONS

▶ What's a zinger?

▶ Why are they fun to hear and read about but not fun to be on the receiving end of?

STRATEGY

1. Share the following:

   Getting along with other technology team members is always a challenge. Too often, team members get in the habit of putting each other down. To help participants understand the importance of human-relation skills, it is sometimes interesting to point out what they are and how they impact people.

2. A zinger is defined as a pointed witty remark or retort. It can be used to cause surprise, shock, or be a good old put-down.

3. One of the most famous was seen in the 1988 campaign debates when Senator Lloyd Bentsen zinged Dan Quayle: "Senator, you're no Jack Kennedy." Quayle's retort was "That was really uncalled for, Senator." Some writers suggested that given what we have learned about the dark side of Jack Kennedy's character—his sexual antics and his cruel use of women—Quayle should have come back with a zinger like: "Having read about Jack Kennedy's true character, I'll take that as a compliment. Thank-you."

4. While we don't like it when people get the best of us, zingers usually lead to more zingers and they can be quite destructive to relationships.

5. For the high political drama situations, zingers may have a place, but when it comes to developing solid team relationships, the best rule of thumb to follow when receiving an insulting remark is to think about a new adage—**better never than late!**

DISCUSSION QUESTIONS

▶ What kind of retorts should be given when you get tossed a cruel insult?

▶ Why has one-upmanship become so prevalent in group interaction—at all levels of human interaction?

Is Your Committee Acting Like a Bunch of Animals?

GOAL

▶ To explore ways of enhancing team communication by focusing on negative examples to identify positive examples.

FOCUS QUESTIONS

▶ How do people act in groups?

▶ Why do some people act positively and others negatively in groups?

STRATEGY

Review "Is Your Committee Acting Like a Bunch of Animals" (see next page). Think about examples of people who have acted out the parts of these animals in previous group situations.

1. Bring a group of participants to the front of the room (eight to ten). Allow them to assume roles of both a trainer and a team member of a group.

2. Write the name of an animal on slips of paper and give to various people. Do not identify the animal to other participants.

3. Select a chairperson who will try to conduct business with the animals.

4. Role-play a situation where some controversial issue is to be discussed and a decision made.

5. Ask other participants who have been watching to identify the different animals that they observed.

6. Debrief team members by asking them how they felt in the role of an animal.

7. Brainstorm strategies for dealing with each animal and insert them next to the animal being discussed (see right-hand column on next page).

NOTE: There is no right or wrong way to deal with animals. However, the teams should be presented with constructive alternatives which range from the most appropriate to the least appropriate.

DISCUSSION QUESTIONS

▶ What did you discover about yourself when you played the role of a team animal?

▶ What is inappropriate response to animal behavior? What is appropriate response to animal behavior?

Is Your Committee Acting Like a Bunch of Animals?

Animal	Strategies for Dealing with Animal
1. Bulls—They charge, attack— often they are abusive, abrupt, and intimidating.	
2. Snakes—They blend in with surroundings and strike suddenly, when you least expect it.	
3. Parrots—They talk and chatter. They sometimes make sense and sometimes not.	
4. Ostriches—They stick their heads in the sand and are noncommittal. They often avoid people.	
5. Rhinoceroses—They are strong, knowledgeable, and they can be described as know-it-alls. Sometimes they are overbearing.	
6. Turkeys—They can't make a decision. They're nice but hope most situations will resolve themselves.	
7. Peacocks—They pretend to be experts, but aren't. They often give wrong or partially correct advice.	

Reducing Negativity Sweetly

GOAL

▶ To reduce the amount of negativity in technology-based learning teams in a humorous fashion.

FOCUS QUESTION

▶ How can we reduce team negativity and focus on the positive?

STRATEGY

A common problem when creating technology-based learning teams is that people sometimes focus on the negative. This is especially detrimental to brainstorming sessions where creativity is paramount.

1. When initially introducing participants to team activities, allot three to five M&Ms or other small pieces of candy to each person.

2. Tell them that there are two rules:

   Rule #1: For every negative statement made, they lose one of their M&Ms.

   Rule #2: For every positive statement, they get to eat one of their M&Ms.

3. Instruct the team facilitator to monitor group activity to ensure rules are adhered to by group members.

4. Discuss follow-up questions at the end of the training session.

NOTE: This activity should be done in a lighthearted fashion to induce humor into the activity. The candy becomes a strong way to deliver the message that we must all be aware of how we react to new ideas.

DISCUSSION QUESTIONS

▶ How did the M&Ms impact your group behavior?
▶ Was this a fun way to keep the group positive?
▶ Who got to eat the greatest number of M&Ms?
▶ Who got most of their M&Ms taken away?
▶ What did you learn about yourself?

□□

Dealing with Difficult People

GOAL

▶ To suggest different strategies when working or dealing with people who are difficult or irritating.

FOCUS QUESTION

▶ How should technology leaders handle difficult people—specifically, those who are highly annoying or unpleasant in the technology-based learning teams?

STRATEGY

1. Relate the following story:

President Lyndon Baines Johnson was well known for his use of off-color language, regardless of the time, place, or audience. Having long desired to rid the Federal Bureau of Investigation of its founding director, J. Edgar Hoover, as many predecessors had unsuccessfully attempted, Johnson became thoroughly annoyed by the difficulties he encountered. Finally resigning himself to Hoover's continued presence, Johnson commented, "It's probably better to have him inside the tent pissing out, than outside pissing in."

NOTE: The off-color language may offend some people. Use with discretion.

DISCUSSION QUESTIONS

▶ How should technology leaders deal with difficult people?
▶ Johnson resigned himself to living with Hoover instead of constantly fighting him. Do you agree that technology leaders should resign themselves to the fact that difficult people will always be present and that we need to bring them inside our tent?
▶ What choices do technology leaders have when dealing with difficult people?

REFERENCE

Adapted from Boone, L.E. (1992). *Quotable Business*. New York: Random House.

Four Dos and Don'ts for Promoting Risk-Taking

GOAL

▶ To explore the leadership role of administrators and technology leaders when working with people.

FOCUS QUESTION

▶ What should building administrators and technology leaders do and not do when working with teachers in the technology staff development program?

STRATEGY

1. Review the following "Four Dos and Don'ts for Promoting Risk-Taking with the Emerging Technologies" (see below).

2. Share the four principles with participants.

3. Allow participants to discuss risk-taking in the technology staff development program.

FOUR DOS AND DON'TS FOR PROMOTING RISK-TAKING WITH THE EMERGING TECHNOLOGIES

1. **Don't** assume the total responsibility for teaching teachers how to use the emerging technologies. Provide resources and support. Then get out of their way! Offer skill training, assistance, and guidance that focuses on improving what they are doing—not evaluating how well they are doing it!

2. **Do** tell teachers it's okay to experiment, make mistakes, and push the edge of the envelope—and mean it.

3. **Do** let teachers find their own answers. Offer a support structure that provides freedom for faculty to express individuality and creativity.

4. **Do** ask questions that push teachers beyond "business as usual thinking." Pose questions like: "What would happen if we tried to link computers with schools across town? Across the nation? Overseas?"

DISCUSSION QUESTIONS

▶ How do these dos and don'ts begin to paint a specific picture of the building administrator as a technology leader?

▶ How is this portrait of leadership different from current styles of administrative leadership?

Five Creativity Blockers

GOAL
▶ To explore ways of encouraging participants to take risks with the emerging technologies by looking at ways that we commonly discourage faculty from taking risks.

FOCUS QUESTION
▶ How can technology leaders encourage participants to take risks with the emerging technologies, and how do we, intentionally or unintentionally, discourage teachers from taking risks?

STRATEGY
Review the summary sheet to familiarize yourself with the five creativity blockers (see next page).

1. Provide a summary sheet relating to the five creativity blockers to participants.

2. Assign two different role-playing situations to students (groups of three to five people).

3. Provide these two different situations to the small groups:

Role-Playing Situation #1: Principal establishes guidelines for supervision of teachers using technology for evaluation purposes—Guidelines: principal will be in room one a week to evaluate; teachers will be rewarded with merit pay for success; faculty will be in competition with other faculty for merit pay.

Role-Playing Situation #2: Principal establishes guidelines for supervision of teachers using technology for experimentation and improvement—Guidelines: principal will be available for help and collaboration of how experimentation may be enhanced; principal supplies resources to support teachers for their effort—equipment , software, etc.; no punishment for failure; encouragement for multiple ways of experimentation with emerging technologies.

DISCUSSION QUESTIONS
▶ How did teachers feel in role-playing situation #1? How did the principal feel? Why?
▶ How did teachers feel in role-playing situation #2? How did the principal feel? Why?
▶ How can technology leaders get teachers to take more risks and enhance their creativity?

REFERENCE
Adapted from Amabile, T. (1992). *Growing Up Creative: Nurturing a Lifetime of Creativity*. Greensboro, NC: Creative Education Fund.

Getting Faculty to Take Risks with the Emerging Technologies

Wherever blockers are strong in technology staff development programs, risk-taking and creativity suffer. The five risk-taking and creativity blockers are:

RISK-TAKING AND CREATIVITY BLOCKER #1: EVALUATION

Teachers are less creative when they are overly focused on how their work is going to be evaluated by the principal.

RISK-TAKING AND CREATIVITY BLOCKER #2: SURVEILLANCE

Teachers are less creative if they fear they are being watched all the time.

RISK-TAKING AND CREATIVITY BLOCKER #3: REWARD

Teachers are most creative when they're doing something for an internal reward—helping kids learn more and be better with technology, or the challenge of redefining teaching and learning, sheer fun of it, etc.

RISK-TAKING AND CREATIVITY BLOCKER #4: COMPETITION

Teachers and adults in general, tend to be less creative and take fewer risks when they find themselves in win-lose situations.

RISK-TAKING AND CREATIVITY BLOCKER #5: RESTRICTED CHOICE

Teachers are generally less creative when they are given little freedom or options when deciding how to do something.

Learning to Fail

GOAL

▶ To illustrate why technology leaders need to embrace failure as a learning process that all technology-based learning teams need to strive for—not as something to be avoided.

FOCUS QUESTIONS

▶ As it relates to the learning process, why is failure good?
▶ What can teachers and technology leaders learn from failure?

STRATEGY

1. Relate the following story:

Thomas Edison (1841–1931) was possibly the world's all-time champion inventor. Edison had only three months' formal education. As a child, he was thought to possibly be retarded. As a consequence, he was taught by his mother and, largely, he was self-taught. He forced himself to look for a second, third, or even fourth answer that he knew would be preferable to the first. Thomas Edison knew 1,800 ways **not** to build a lightbulb. Yet he had more than 1,300 U.S. and foreign patents. Edison knew that failure was a prerequisite to success. Edison learned how to fail and how to learn from his failures.

2. Direct the group to think about failure and what they are doing with the emerging technologies.

3. Can we expect to have failure when we are experimenting with the emerging technologies?

DISCUSSION QUESTIONS

▶ Why do we fear failure?
▶ Why is "screwing up" punished more than rewarded in schools?
▶ Does society reward people for failure?
▶ What can technology leaders and teachers learn from people like Edison?

The Importance of Learning to Fail

GOAL

▶ To illustrate why technology leaders need to embrace failure as a learning process that needs to be encouraged in technology-based learning teams—not something to be avoided.

FOCUS QUESTIONS

▶ As it relates to individual learning, why is failure good?
▶ What can teachers and technology leaders learn from failure?

STRATEGY

1. Relate the following:

   Historical events have many examples of failures that generated new solutions. For example:

   Problem: Meltdown of nuclear reactor at Three-Mile Island—1979.
   New Solution: This led to new regulations and safety features on building nuclear power plants.

   Problem: Wreck of Supertanker Exxon Valdez—1989.
   New Solution: This led to new safety features of oil tankers and regulations of shipping oil.

   Problem: Explosion of *Challenger* space shuttle—1983.
   New Solution: This led to new safety features of space travel.

2. Now, we could argue that these events shouldn't have happened at all. People's lives should not have been lost and the environment should not have been destroyed, but these failures did lead to something better! **Failure is a prerequisite to learning.**

3. Have participants list three other historical events that illustrate how failure can and should lead to new solutions, successes, and improvements.

DISCUSSION QUESTIONS

▶ What events in your own life illustrate that you have learned how to fail?
▶ Why aren't our current instructional, learning, and assessment practices conducive to having students learn from failure?

Lessons from Failure

GOAL

▶ To illustrate what lessons can be learned from failure and apply them to technology experimentation.

FOCUS QUESTIONS

▶ What have you learned from failure in school?

▶ What have you learned from failure in life?

▶ What can we learn from failure when we experience it in the technology staff development program?

STRATEGY

1. Get participants to list failures that they have had in school or in their lives. Share them.

2. Have participants talk about who they learned from (e.g., parent, teacher, brother, sister, etc.). Talk about them.

3. Have participants tell what lessons they have learned from failure.

4. Take "Lessons from Failure" audit (see next page).

DISCUSSION QUESTIONS

▶ Why does it feel bad to fail?

▶ Should we feel bad when we fail?

▶ How has our education prepared us for failure?

▶ How will fear of failure keep us from realizing the true potential of technology as a tool to transform education?

▶ If few "lessons" come out in the discussion, use the following ideas to generate additional ideas:

FAILURE

▶ Fear of failure keeps us from generating new ideas.

▶ People need to look at failure as a learning process.

▶ Many of our more important discoveries were based on some initial failure that led to a new way of thinking.

▶ Our current grading system sets us up for failure but does not teach us what to learn from failure.

Lessons from Failure

___T ___F **1.** Failure is good.

___T ___F **2.** I like to try new things.

___T ___F **3.** It is embarrassing to make mistakes in public.

___T ___F **4.** Our educational system is based on the "right answers," which teaches students to think conservatively.

___T ___F **5.** The following is representative of our grading system:

> A = 90% of the time you are right
>
> B = 80% of the time you are right
>
> C = 70% of the time you are right
>
> D = 60% of the time you are right
>
> F = Anything less than 60%—**YOU FAIL**

___T ___F **6.** When I make an error, it makes me feel bad.

___T ___F **7.** I put myself in situations where there is a risk of failing.

___T ___F **8.** Education should teach people how to fail intelligently.

___T ___F **9.** Education should teach people to keep trying and failing until they learn what works.

___T ___F **10.** Great thinkers and inventors of the past knew how to fail.

___T ___F **11.** The grading system adequately reflects what students know.

___T ___F **12.** Failure is bad.

___T ___F **13.** Productive living and citizenship involve failing.

SCORING: There are no right or wrong answers. The quiz is intended to make you think about failure in a more positive light. Share your opinions with others.

Self-Handicapping and Avoiding Failure

GOAL
▶ To help participants understand why people engage in self-defeating behavior.

FOCUS QUESTION
▶ How can we encourage people to become more aware of self-handicapping when experimenting with the emerging technologies?

STRATEGY

1. Share the following information:
   ▶ **Definition:** *Self-handicapping* is a form of self-defeating (self-sabotaging) behavior or, in plain terms, excuse-making.
   ▶ **Explanation:** By taking on a handicap, a person makes it more likely that he or she will fail at an endeavor. Two psychologists, Berglas and Baumeister, say this is a clever trick of the mind where one sets up a win-win situation by allowing him- or herself to save face when he or she does fail.
   ▶ **Historical Self-Handicapper:** A classic example is the French chess champion Deschapelles, who lived during the 18th century. Deschapelles was a phenomenal player who quickly became champion of his region. But when competition grew tougher, he adopted a new condition for all matches. He would compete only if his opponent would remove one of Deschapelles's pawns and make the first move, increasing the odds that Deschapelles would lose. If he did lose, he could blame it on the other player's advantage; but if he won against such odds, he would be all the more revered for his amazing talents. Psychologists now use the term "Deschappelles's coup" to refer to acts of self-sabotage rampant in today's world.
   ▶ **Other Facts:** (1) More men than women engage in self-handicapping. (2) Ironically, it is often success that leads people to flirt with failure. (3) Those obsessed with success are chronic excuse-makers. (4) People are so afraid of being labeled a failure at anything that they constantly develop one handicap or another in order to explain away failure. (5) Over the long run, excuse-makers fail to live up to their true potential, thwart their own goals, and lose the status they care so much about.

DISCUSSION QUESTIONS
▶ Do you know colleagues that engage in self-handicapping? Students?
▶ Have you ever engaged in self-handicapping?
▶ Since risk-taking is critical to the success of the technology staff development program, how can we use this knowledge to deal with or prevent self-handicapping?

REFERENCE
Adapted from Berglas, S. & Baumeister, R. (1993). *Your Own Worst Enemy.*
New York: Basic Books.

Have You Tried These Technology-Based Learning Methods?

GOALS

► To illustrate the different kinds of teaching and learning methodologies that are possible with emerging technologies.

► To illustrate the different kinds of teaching and learning methodologies that should be modeled in a technology staff development program.

FOCUS QUESTIONS

► What are technology-based learning methods?

► What makes these methods different from traditional methods of lecture, inquiry, small-group instruction, cooperative learning, etc.?

STRATEGY

1. Ask participants if they are aware of any technology-based learning methods.

2. Depending on responses, circulate definitions of the ten technology-based learning methodologies (see next page).

3. Discuss the various models and implications for teaching and learning.

4. Ask participants if they have ever used or seen one or more of the technology-based learning methodologies demonstrated.

5. Determine the feasibility of technology-based learning methods when compared with traditional teaching and learning methods.

6. Ask participants to prepare a plan which describes how they might begin to explore one or more of the technology-based learning methodologies.

7. Ask participants to generate additional technology-based learning methodologies.

DISCUSSION QUESTIONS

► Why are the technology-based learning methods powerful?

► Are they more powerful than conventional teaching methodologies? Why or why not?

Ten Technology-Based Learning Methods

1. **Teacher-Talk with Text and Technology**—Teacher talk with textbook as center of learning but computer software or other technology used in classroom interaction/demonstration for drill-and-practice and/or remediation and/or assessment.

2. **Integrated Learning Systems or ILSs**—Complex, integrated hardware/software management systems using computer-based instruction. General characteristics include the following: instructional objectives specified with individual lessons tied to the objectives; lessons integrated into the standard curriculum; courseware that spans several grade levels in comprehensive fashion—courseware delivered on a networked system of microcomputers or terminals with color graphics and sound; and management system which collects and records results of student performance.

3. **Multimedia Learning**—Teacher and students using multimedia computing, where the machine architecture has the ability to input, manipulate, and output graphics, audio, and video.

4. **Electronic Cooperative Learning**—Students working together—electronically—to achieve a common learning goal by using technology. There are four essential elements in an effective cooperative lesson: positive interdependence, individual accountability, interpersonal and small-group skills, and group processing. Face-to-face interaction, which is typically associated with cooperative learning, is not an essential feature of electronic cooperative learning.

5. **Electronic Collaborative Learning**—Larger number of students working together on a single project or product. Students usually have their own computer and other emerging technologies but are networked, which allows them to focus on one project or product simultaneously.

6. **Computer Lab/Networked Lab**—Students using computers for drill-and-practice based on individual software; computers used for experimentation and exploration tied to student needs; sometimes connected and sometimes independent of standard curriculum.

7. **Hypertext/Hypermedia**—Teacher and/or student creates or uses multilayered text with connecting links which include graphics, sound, and video.

8. **Electronic Gaming Simulation**—Student learning through use of software which emulates real-world activities and occurrences.

9. **Electronic Distance Learning**—Use of computer and modem by students to communicate with other students, experts, databases, etc.

10. **Virtual Reality**—Exploration of artificial worlds existing only in the computer's electronic circuitry by using computer-linked gloves and goggles.

Build a Set of Technology Team Guidelines!

GOAL

▶ To foster team-building skills by creating a set of technology team guidelines.

FOCUS QUESTION

▶ Can teams come together to develop guidelines that will help them build more effective, efficient technology teams?

STRATEGY

1. Divide the group into teams of four to six people. Explain that the premise of this exercise is to build a series of statements that represent guidelines for directing the team's activities.

2. Have individual groups report their guidelines to the larger group. After all groups have reported, show them the guidelines entitled, "A Strategy for Effective Teamwork!" (see next page). Ask them to compare how many of their guidelines match this information. It is not imperative that they match exactly, but it does give participants additional ideas for identifying group guidelines.

3. When discussion is completed, have the groups rate themselves (as a group) concerning how well they have been following these guidelines throughout the project.

DISCUSSION QUESTIONS

▶ Did you use the guidelines that you developed as the activity was occurring?
▶ Were you acting like a team even before you identified specific team guidelines?
▶ How can you ensure that your team will use these guidelines in the future?

RESOURCE

Adapted from Wilson, P. (December 22, 1992). Teamwork takes on new dimension in '90s. *The Kansas City Star*.

A Strategy for Effective Teamwork!

Leadership skills that build strong teams are sometimes missing in the American culture and we frequently praise only those individuals who have characteristics like the movie character Rambo.

In order to provide individuals with the necessary tools for developing good team dynamics, facilitators need to help participants develop strong leadership principles. Some of these include:

1. **Shared vision—** the idea that a common goal and the ability to articulate this goal becomes the linking factor between a group of people working together and a team.

2. **Defined expectations—** putting limits on and assigning specific duties to team members is important. The purpose is to define the boundaries in such a way as to allow creativity to exist but at the same time avoid duplication of efforts. Team members need a clear picture of what is expected of them.

3. **Measuring devices—** specific performance goals are identified for the entire team. These goals can identify "contributing to the success of other team members;" thereby allowing a competitive outlook to be replaced by a cooperative attitude.

4. **Regular practice—** provides the team with regularly scheduled meetings so that they might practice their teamwork skills, become better acquainted, and understand group strengths and weaknesses. Within regular practice, team learning is the key to making the team functional. The skills of problem solving and working together are all nurtured by the environment. Teams must practice new roles, shifting from key players to supportive allies.

STAGE 4

Institutionalizing Technology Staff Development Programs

Storytelling—The Culture of Technology

GOAL

▶ To understand the importance of passing on culture and giving ownership to participants when implementing technology staff development programs.

FOCUS QUESTION

▶ Why is it important to involve all stakeholders in creating the history or culture of the technology staff development program?

STRATEGY

1. Facilitator should begin a story. Try to make the story relevant to a specific technology idea you are trying to convey. Then, in the middle of the story, select someone in the group to continue the story. This individual should then take the story by adding his or her own interesting touches—as long as it relates to technology. Then have that person point to another group member to continue the story.

2. If you have a specific ending in mind, the story should end with facilitator talking about the technology story.

DISCUSSION QUESTIONS

▶ What was the impact of involving several people when telling a story?
▶ What are the implications of this activity for planning and implementing a technology staff development program?

Shaping a Technology Culture

GOAL

▶ To think about how to build a strong culture around the technology staff development program.

FOCUS QUESTION

▶ How can writing, telling, and sharing stories enhance your technology staff development program and school's culture?

STRATEGY

1. Talk to participants about the importance of culture and a feeling of belonging.

2. Relate the following:

    Every culture around the world is conveyed through powerful ideas such as telling stories. Stories make deep impressions. Think of the great religious books of all time: the Bible, the Koran, Buddha's written sayings, etc.

3. Examine the suggested strategies for writing and telling stories (see next page).

4. Have participants write some of these stories.

DISCUSSION QUESTIONS

▶ Why are stories important to the cohesiveness of the technology staff development teams? The total technology staff development program?

▶ How do you feel when stories are told?

▶ What is the power of storytelling?

REFERENCE

Adapted from Armstrong, D. (1992). *Managing by Storying Around*. New York: Doubleday.

Shaping a Technology Culture

1. Start to think of the technology staff development program in a new way. Visualize the program and people not as individuals with whom you work but as a tribe, knitted together by common values.

2. Every tribe has its stories that teach newcomers what it means to belong. The morals of these stories are always clear. These stories are found in many religious documents such as the Bible, the Koran, etc. and often contain metaphors.

3. Make a list of the core values that represent the technology staff development program. These are "tribe values" that are held dear (e.g., student-centered learning through technology; technology as an empowerment tool; learning anything, anytime, anywhere; etc.). Think of an occasion when a teacher or administrator strikingly lived up to (or violated) one of those values. Write it up as a story with a moral. Do that for each of your program's core values.

4. Always begin with a heroic deed that you witnessed or that teachers told you about.

5. Make sure the story is true. Verify all information and facts.

6. Think of a clever title for the story.

7. Stick to one idea or theme in the story.

8. Keep the story short. No longer than one, single-spaced typed page, or two to five minutes orally.

9. Schedule a meeting for celebration activities—where the story or stories are told and exchanged.

10. Frame the original and give it to the people mentioned in the story as a form of recognition.

11. Most importantly, use the storytelling activity as a celebration activity and not as a reward which is used as external motivation.

NOTE: The technology staff development program must be the source of the stories and the stories must exemplify the virtues the group believes in and intends to pursue.

Adapted from Armstrong, D. (1992). *Managing by Storying Around*. New York: Doubleday.

Create Your History by Building a Technology Game!

GOAL
▶ To learn facts about an organization and build a culture (stories) that can be shared with others.

FOCUS QUESTIONS
▶ What do we know about our technology staff development program?

▶ How can we preserve this information so that it can be transmitted to others over time?

STRATEGY
Relate to the group that they are going to build a game that reflects the history of the technology staff development program.

1. Divide into teams of four to six.

2. Distribute a stack of index cards for each group.

3. Provide the following directions: For each card, write a question that relates to the technology staff development program or a person involved in the technology staff development program. Option: Transpose these materials to HyperCard or LinkWay Live.

4. Identify questions like:
    a. When was the program initiated? (date)
    b. Who was responsible for organizing the program?
    c. What kind of equipment was first used? (list equipment)
    d. Who were some of the original pioneers with the emerging technologies?

5. Then have participants create a technology game board which allows movement of players from starting point to ending point. Include a die which directs players to spaces on the board.

6. Have different teams update the technology game over time.

7. Have teams play the game periodically when new members are brought into the teams.

DISCUSSION QUESTIONS
▶ What value is there to telling stories about your technology staff development program?

▶ Does the technology game have long-term historical value? Why?

Find a Good Wing to Climb Under!

GOAL

▶ To explore power of mentoring when creating effective technology staff development programs.

FOCUS QUESTIONS

▶ How can technology-literate mentors help you become a team member and teacher?

▶ Can mentors make a difference in your professional life?

▶ How can technology-literate mentors transform your professional life?

STRATEGY

1. Share the following information:

   Mentoring is about someone sharing information with someone else in a personal way. Most successful people have had strong mentors who cultivated their talents and helped them get "breaks."

   Mentors offer access to opportunities and insight, and teach valuable lessons. While corporations often offer mentoring programs, it is less common in education.

   In technology staff development programs, people need to seek out mentors even though they have not been officially sanctioned.

   But how do you unlock the mysteries of mentoring?

2. At this point, share or provide the information labeled "Unlocking the Treasure Chest of Mentoring" (see next page).

3. Get participants to discuss mentoring and its implications for transforming schools with the emerging technologies.

4. Have participants discuss strategies for identifying mentors or becoming mentors to others.

5. Have participants develop a profile of a "perfect" technology-literate mentor.

6. Have participants contact a potential mentor and schedule their first meeting.

DISCUSSION QUESTIONS

▶ How can mentoring facilitate the technology staff development program?

▶ Have you ever had a mentor?

▶ What personal experiences can you share about mentoring?

Unlocking the Treasure Chest of Mentoring

1. **Seek Opportunity.** Choose your mentor wisely by selecting someone who:
   - is competent when using technology;
   - believes in you;
   - has time to work with you when you are working with technology; and
   - has the technology skills you need.

2. **Employ a Variety of Strategies for Selecting a Mentor.** Try to:
   - ask for that person's advice;
   - volunteer to help that person; and
   - provide information that will assist that person.

3. **Be Willing to Learn.** To find a mentor, you must be open to new challenges. Openness to learning new things is not always easy. Try to:
   - ask lots of questions without "bugging" that person;
   - spend time around that person when he or she is working with technology; and
   - take risks with the technology that show your eagerness to make a difference.

4. **Be Willing to Give Back.** For a mentor-mentee relationship to work, it must be reciprocal. Strategies for "paying back" include trying to:
   - show openness when discussing new ideas;
   - show loyalty and trustworthiness; and
   - provide relief when that person is under stress.

5. **Show Your Gratitude.** The person who has a mentor exhibits appreciation by his or her own success. Strategies for saying "thanks" include:
   - thanking your mentor regularly—sincerely;
   - talking about the importance of your mentor relationship with that person;
   - sharing technology successes with each other; and
   - becoming a technology-literate mentor to other people.

What's Your Team's PR Quotient?

GOAL

▶ To enhance technology team members' understanding of public relations and the influence of publicity on technology integration and the technology staff development program.

FOCUS QUESTION

▶ Why is public relations so important to innovations of technology integration?

STRATEGY

Share with participants the importance of good publicity—both internal and external.

1. Some general rules to following when publicizing your achievements are:

   a. Be very positive. Any negative statement can be taken out of context. Make sure your sound bytes reflect well on you.

   b. Be on the offensive rather than the defensive. If a reporter asks you about the high costs of the emerging technologies, say, "I'm glad that you asked that because parents and the community need to understand that the continual upgrading of equipment is needed in order to give students a realistic picture of the technology that they will be using in the business world."

   c. Use all the media. Seek out coverage from all of your local newspapers and radio stations, and the school paper. Get your message out by using many different channels.

2. Divide the group into teams of four to six. Allow them to assume roles of both a reporter and a team member supplying information.

   Situation #1: Reporter asks embarrassing question.

   Situation #2: Board of education requests an explanation of why only one school is receiving publicity about its use of technology.

   Situation #3: Local radio does a phone interview and begins to focus on the lack of research concerning emerging technologies and student learning.

3. Allow teams to discuss role-playing situations.

DISCUSSION QUESTIONS

▶ What did you discover about yourself in an interviewer-interviewee situation?

▶ How important is public relations when you are dealing with innovations such as the emerging technologies?

Grades and Technology Integration

GOAL

▶ To illustrate the importance of human creativity and the danger of "right-way thinking" when integrating technology in education.

FOCUS QUESTIONS

▶ How do grades impact student creativity?

▶ How do teachers typically view any kind of deviation from the "right answers"?

STRATEGY

1. Relate the following story:

   A teacher assigned her students to color a picture that has a scene including a house, a tree, grass, flowers, and sky. All students are instructed to use appropriate colors in the assignment.

   The teacher returns the graded papers. Almost all students who followed instructions received a passing grade.

   There are three exceptions, however; Brook, Morgana, and Gwen.

   a. Brook got a failing grade because she colored outside the lines of the scene—intentionally.

   b. Morgana got a failing grade because she colored outside the lines of the scene—unintentionally.

   c. Gwen got a failing grade because she colored the house light gray, the grass dark gray, the flowers black, and the sky yellow.

2. Now ask the group whether the passing and failing grades assigned by the teacher were justified and why.

3. Now tell them about Gwen. When quizzed about not using the "right" colors, Gwen responded that she chose to use the colors she did because her house looked like this in the early hours before dawn.

DISCUSSION QUESTIONS

▶ What lesson did Gwen learn? Morgana? Brook?

▶ Should the teacher have learned a lesson? What? Why?

▶ What does this assignment and grading system tell us about our teaching and learning paradigms?

▶ Is there a lesson to be learned about how we assess the impact of learning when we allow students to use the emerging technologies?

Student Assessment and Multiple Intelligences

GOAL

▶ To illustrate that different intelligences require different forms of student assessment measures—especially when using the emerging technologies.

FOCUS QUESTIONS

▶ How do we assess students under our current system of education?

▶ How should we evaluate student performance when we take the seven forms of intelligences into consideration?

STRATEGY

1. Ask participants if they are aware of the seven intelligences identified and investigated by Howard Gardner.

2. Based on their responses, circulate the definitions and examples of the seven intelligences (see next page).

3. Discuss the seven intelligences and corresponding assessment measures required to measure those intelligences.

DISCUSSION QUESTION

▶ What happening or innovation will it take to move away from traditional assessment measures which typically deal with linguistic and logical-mathematical intelligences?

RESOURCES

Armstrong, T. (1993). *7 Kinds of Smart—Identifying and Developing Your Many Intelligences.* New York: Plume.

Gardner, H. (1983). *Frames of Mind: The Theory of Multiple Intelligences.* New York: Basic Books.

Student Assessment and Multiple Intelligences

1. **Linguistic Intelligence**
   Definition: intelligence of words
   Occupations: journalist, storyteller, poet, and lawyer
   Famous people: Shakespeare, Homer, Maya Angelou, etc.
   Skills: writing, retaining factual information, etc.

2. **Logical-Mathematical Intelligence**
   Definition: intelligence of numbers and logic
   Occupations: scientist, accountant, and computer programmer
   Famous people: Newton, Einstein, Stephen Hawking, etc.
   Skills: reasoning, seeing cause-and-effect relationships, seeing numerical patterns, etc.

3. **Spatial Intelligence**
   Definition: thinking in pictures and images and the ability to perceive, transform, and re-create different aspects of the visual-spatial world
   Occupations: architect, photographer, artist, pilot, and mechanical engineer
   Famous People: Edison, Pablo Picasso, Ansel Adams, etc.
   Skills: acute sensitivity to visual details, drawing, sketching, etc.

4. **Musical Intelligence**
   Definition: capacity to perceive, appreciate, and produce rhythms and melodies
   Occupations: musician, etc.
   Famous People: Bach, Beethoven, Brahms, the Beatles, I. Pearlman, etc.
   Skills: singing, keeping time, listening with discernment

5. **Bodily-Kinesthetic Intelligence**
   Definition: intelligence of the physical self
   Occupations: athlete, craftsperson, mechanic, and surgeon
   Famous People: Jim Thorpe, Charlie Chaplin, Jackie Joyner, etc.
   Skills: athleticism, tactile sensitivity, "hands-on" activities

6. **Interpersonal Intelligence**
   Definition: ability to understand and work with other people
   Occupations: politician, social director, corporation executive
   Famous People: Mahatma Gandhi, Machiavelli, Lyndon Baines Johnson, etc.
   Skills: networking, negotiating, teaching

7. **Intrapersonal Intelligence**
   Definition: ability to accept personal feelings, to discriminate between many different kinds of inner-emotional states, and to use self-understanding to enrich and guide life
   Occupations: counselor, theologian, self-employed businessperson
   Famous People: Billy Graham, Dr. Ruth, Dave Thomas, etc.
   Skills: working independently

Adapted from Armstrong, T. (1993). *7 Kinds of Smart—Identifying and Developing Your Many Intelligences.* New York: Plume.

Tell Me About It!

GOAL

▶ To provide technology staff development participants with an opportunity to give feedback about training, trainer, and self.

FOCUS QUESTIONS

▶ What did you learn today?

▶ What do you still need to learn?

▶ What was the quality of training?

▶ What did you bring to the training session?

STRATEGY

1. Provide participants with a feedback sheet (see next page).

2. Provide the following directions and instructions:

    You are being asked to provide feedback about the training sessions and trainer.

    a. This feedback will not be examined until all participant evaluations are completed.

    b. Do not put your name on the sheet.

    c. Print if you wish to disguise handwriting.

    d. This feedback will be used to improve trainer behavior.

    e. This feedback will be used to improve training program for subsequent participants.

    f. When you have completed the form, turn the sheet facedown and place it on the desk.

DISCUSSION QUESTIONS

▶ What could we do to improve the quality of training?

▶ What general suggestions do you have?

▶ Did you feel comfortable or uncomfortable when providing feedback?

□□□

Feedback

Date: _____

Location: _____

Training Session/Topic: _____

1. Write three words (single words or phrases) that describe this training session:

    A. _____

    B. _____

    C. _____

2. Write three words (single words or phrases) that describe the trainer:

    A. _____

    B. _____

    C. _____

3. Write three words (single words or phrases) that describe your efforts—the amount of work you put into the training program:

    A. _____

    B. _____

    C. _____

4. Overall, I would rank this training session as: (circle one)

    A. Excellent

    B. Above Average

    C. Average

    D. Below Average

5. Overall, I would rank the trainer's performance as: (circle one)

    A. Excellent

    B. Above Average

    C. Average

    D. Below Average

6. Overall, I would rank my learning or achievement in this training session as: (circle one)

    A. Excellent

    B. Above Average

    C. Average

    D. Below Average

Fishbowling

GOAL

► To provide an opportunity to make suggestions for improving technology training and learning.

FOCUS QUESTION

► How can fishbowling help us improve the technology training session?

STRATEGY

1. Relate the following:

   Fishbowling is a term given to a strategy that allows participants to provide feedback to the trainer and other participants. The term means to "get out of the fishbowl and look back at where you have been swimming." It is only when you process what you have done that you can plan for the next session.

2. Announce that fishbowling will occur at the end of every training session, and will last anywhere from five to fifteen minutes (longer if necessary).

3. Instruct participants that any of the following questions can and should be addressed:
   How did you feel about the technology training today?
   What went well?
   What could we do better?
   What should we do differently?
   What are my needs?

4. Remind participants that honesty and forthrightness are required. This should not be a threatening exercise for participants or trainer. The goal is to produce a dialogue that allows the training process to get better as it progresses.

NOTE: This activity will only work when the technology trainer uses this as an improvement activity and not as a complaint session. Participants should not be punished for blunt responses about the training or trainer. Most importantly, the technology trainer should be prepared for both positive and negative feedback. Remember, the purpose of the activity is group improvement, group progress, and group rapport. If this activity does not produce these outcomes, discontinue it and use a more anonymous form of feedback.

DISCUSSION QUESTIONS

► How do you feel about fishbowling?
► Is fishbowling threatening to you?
► What are the advantages and disadvantages to fishbowling?

Anonymous Fishbowling

GOAL

▶ To provide an opportunity for technology participants to express individual problems or concerns.

FOCUS QUESTION

▶ How can we use anonymous fishbowling to help us improve technology training sessions?

STRATEGY

1. Relate the following:
   Anonymous fishbowling is a term given to a strategy that allows participants to provide feedback to the trainer and other participants.

2. Announce that participants will now have a chance to "put their problem in a fishbowl."

3. Provide time at the beginning or end of the training session for participants to air (in writing) their concerns, questions, or problems by writing them down on a slip of paper.

4. After writing the question, direct participants to place the papers in the fishbowl.

5. Reserve a time at the beginning or end of the training session to draw the slips of paper out of the fishbowl.

6. The trainer can either address the issue him- or herself or form teams to address the concern(s). Participants who have the same concern, question, or problem can be allowed time to engage in discussion by forming a small group.

7. Remind participants that honesty is required and that this is not a complaint session. The goal of this activity is to produce a dialogue among participants which allows the training process to get better.

NOTE: This activity will only work when the trainer uses this as an improvement exercise and not as a complaint session.

DISCUSSION QUESTIONS

▶ How do you feel about anonymous fishbowling?
▶ Can anonymous fishbowling be helpful to us?
▶ What are the advantages and disadvantages to anonymous fishbowling?

Planned Abandonment and Emerging Technologies

GOAL

▶ To show that the emerging technologies can help in planned-abandonment practices.

FOCUS QUESTION

▶ How can the emerging technologies help in eliminating outdated practices (e.g., school practices, teaching practices, learning procedures, etc.)?

STRATEGY

1. Divide the group into three teams.

2. Participants can be assigned or volunteer to work in one of three areas: (a) schools, (b) teaching, or (c) learning.

3. Instruct the group to write down current practices that are required to maintain maximum educational efficiency and effectiveness.

4. Now instruct the group to write down current practices that have been made obsolete by the emerging technologies (or at least improved by using the emerging technologies).

5. After the lists are compiled, identify those practices which are obsolete and eliminated. Specify those practices which could be improved. Specify those current practices that cannot be eliminated or improved by the emerging technologies.

DISCUSSION QUESTIONS

▶ How well have schools kept up with planned abandonment as it relates to the use of emerging technologies?

▶ How can planned abandonment improve education?

How Should We Communicate?

GOAL

▶ Determining which forms of communication are most effective when publicizing events and activities related to technology staff development programs.

FOCUS QUESTIONS

▶ In relation to our technology staff development program, how do we communicate with our stakeholders?

▶ Which forms of communication should be a priority?

STRATEGY

1. Divide into small groups.

2. Discuss the importance of communication and public relations concerning technology integration programs.

3. Brainstorm the methods of communication (e.g., news article; one-on-one, face-to-face communication, etc.).

4. Compare the new list to the "Hierarchy of Effective Communication" (see next page).

DISCUSSION QUESTION

▶ Develop a priority list of the communication methods that you will use in the future to publicize your technology staff development program.

REFERENCE

Adapted from *pr reporter*, August 1991 and *ViewPOINT*, Colorado Association of School Executives, December, 1992.

Hierarchy of Effective Communication—From Most Effective to Least Effective

1. One-on-one, face-to-face

2. Small-group discussion/meeting

3. Speaking before a large group

4. Phone conversation

5. Handwritten personal note

6. Typewritten personal letter, not generated by a computer

7. Computer-generated or word-processing generated personal letter

8. Mass-produced, nonpersonal letter

9. Brochure or pamphlet sent out as a direct-mail piece

10. Article in organizational newsletter, magazine, tabloid

11. News carried in popular press

12. Advertising in newspapers, radio, TV, magazines, posters, etc.

13. Other forms of communications (billboards, skywriters, etc.)

STAGE 5

Special Activities for Situations and Trainers

Technology Is My Bag!

GOAL

▶ Get acquainted with others in the technology staff development program by equating yourself with the emerging technologies.

FOCUS QUESTION

▶ What technological innovation best describes you and why?

STRATEGY

1. Instruct the group that they are going to get acquainted by selecting a piece of technology that best represents their personal characteristics. Examples might include: a computer, laser videodisc, CD-ROM, satellite, copy machine, VCR, LCD panel (liquid crystal display), overhead projector, laser-disc player, television, fax, modem, telephone, or answering machine.

2. Allow participants to explore and analyze their selections with other participants.

3. List the selections on a flip chart, board, or computer/LCD panel.

DISCUSSION QUESTIONS

▶ What characteristics did you share in common with the emerging technology that you selected?

▶ Can others in your group add to the characteristics that you've identified? Can you add to other characteristics?

▶ What did you learn about the other people in your group? What were they surprised to learn about you?

Technology Is Nothing to Sneeze At!

GOAL

▶ To provide an opening exercise for a technology staff development activity and place participants at ease in a humorous fashion.

FOCUS QUESTION

▶ Is technology something to sneeze at?

STRATEGY

1. Divide group into threes.

2. Ask first group to say *Hishee* with emphasis on *shee*.

3. Ask second group to say *Hoshee* with emphasis on *shee*.

4. Ask third group to say *Hashee* with emphasis on *shee*.

5. After each group has practiced saying their word in unison on the count of three, have all three group say their words together.

6. This should sound like a large sneeze. You respond with "Bless You." And begin your presentation or talk with: "Technology is nothing to sneeze at."

DISCUSSION QUESTION

▶ None necessary.

REFERENCE

Adapted from *Reader's Digest* (ed). (1971). *Book of 1,000 Family Games*. Pleasantville, New York: The Reader's Digest Association, Inc.

Sitting Up

GOAL

▶ Get technology staff development participants involved and ready to begin a new activity.

FOCUS QUESTION

▶ How do we have some fun and get some exercise at the same time?

STRATEGY

1. Read the following to group from a flip chart or computer/LCD panel:

Hands on your hips, hands on your knees
Put them behind you if you please.
Touch your shoulders, touch your nose
Touch your ears, touch your toes.

Raise your hands high in the air
At your sides, on your hair.
Raise you hands as before,
While you clap, one, two, three, four.

My hands upon my head I place
On my shoulders, on my face.
Then I raise them up on high
And make my fingers quickly fly.

Then I put them in front of me,
And gently clap them one, two, three.

2. Then let group laugh and talk before getting ready to move on to next activity.

DISCUSSION QUESTION

▶ None necessary.

Technology Puzzle

GOAL

▶ To facilitate technology staff participants getting to know each other by putting together a piece or a page from any technology manual. (**NOTE:** Participants may need to read the page and understand its content before they can puzzle it together with others.)

FOCUS QUESTION

▶ How do we get acquainted?

STRATEGY

1. Take a page from your technology staff development sourcebook or a picture of a piece of technology equipment. Cut the picture or page into puzzlelike pieces. Each participant is given a piece of the puzzle upon entering the room. The object of the exercise is to have them circulate around the room until they have all pieces of their puzzle together.

2. While doing this exercise, participants should be instructed to find out who they are working with.

DISCUSSION QUESTIONS

▶ Did you have to read the page before you could put the puzzle together?
▶ How well did you get to know other people? Why or why not?

How Well Can You Catch?

GOAL

▶ To set the stage of the technology workshop in a fun fashion by playing catch.

FOCUS QUESTION

▶ How can we make each other comfortable and at the same time learn something?

STRATEGY

1. A common problem when setting the stage for the technology training session is that the trainer may not know very much about his or her audience. Sometimes it is awkward or mundane to find out everyone's name by merely having them introduce themselves. As a consequence, the trainer often speeds ahead and fails to tailor the message and activities to the individual needs of participants.

2. To become more familiar with your audience, tell the group that you're glad to be here but you need to know more about them. Briefly begin by introducing yourself and then toss a rubber ball to a participant who must announce his or her name and occupation specialty. However, there are two rules.

   Rule #1: If anyone drops the ball, they must relate a secret about him- or herself that no one else knows. The secret must be truly a secret—until now!

   Rule #2: The ball must be thrown across the room and not just tossed.

NOTE: This activity should occur very rapidly and works well with a limited number of participants. With large numbers, divide participants in groups of eight to ten. Sometimes it is helpful to have some participants "planted in audience" who are instructed to intentionally throw the ball so that it can not be caught—forcing the unsuspecting person to reveal secrets.

DISCUSSION QUESTION

▶ None necessary.

Stressed Out?

GOAL

▶ To think about specific ways to decrease your physical tension and mental stress during technology staff development program activities.

FOCUS QUESTION

▶ How can we use stress-relief stretches to help people become more relaxed when working in technology staff development activities?

STRATEGY

1. Talk to participants about the importance of knowing how to relax.

2. Use a variety of exercises (see next page).

3. Teach different strategies over a period of time.

4. Intersperse regular activities with stress-reliever stretches whenever possible.

DISCUSSION QUESTIONS

▶ Why is it important that we learn to relax during intense technology staff development activities?

▶ What causes tension in the workplace?

▶ Do these stress-relieving activities help?

REFERENCE

Adapted from Friedeberger, J. (1992) *Office Yoga: Tackling Tension with Simple Stretches You Can Do at Your Desk*. San Francisco: Thorsons SF.

Try Stress-Relief Stretches!

If the pressures of staff development have been getting you down lately, take a few minutes to think about specific ways to decrease your physical tension and mental stress. First get into the right mind-set and position.

GENERAL RELAXATION:

▶ Sit up straight. Drop your shoulders back and let your arms hang loosely. This takes the strain off your back and allows your lungs and other organs to function correctly.

▶ Breathe deeply. Deep, slow, rhythmic breathing has a calming effect.

▶ Take a mental vacation. Close your eyes and breathe deeply—recall a time when you were calm and happy. Place yourself into the scene in your mind.

Now try the following stretches as often as possible to help relieve stress.

RELAX SHOULDERS AND CHEST:

▶ With arms hanging at sides, gently circle shoulders forward, then backward.

▶ Slowly lift shoulders while inhaling, and then slowly drop shoulders while exhaling.

▶ Place fingertips on shoulders. Bring elbows together in front of your chest and lift them. Then allow elbows to swing open.

LOOSEN NECK MUSCLES:

▶ Tilt head back looking toward the ceiling, then down toward chest.

▶ Turn head to look over right shoulder, then back to the front. Repeat with left shoulder.

LIMBER LEGS:

▶ While sitting, straighten and stiffen right leg to the front and push heel away so the back of the leg is stretched. Repeat with left leg.

▶ While legs are straightened to the front, circle feet to relax ankle muscles.

EASE BACK TENSION:

▶ With fingers laced together in front, push palms away. Raise straightened arms above head, palms to ceiling. Lower linked hands to behind your head. Move elbows and shoulders back until you feel the stretch of muscles in arms and upper back. Stretch arms up, palms to ceiling.

▶ Sitting straight up with hands placed on lower back, slowly arch back and look upward toward ceiling, breathing deeply. Then, with hands still on your back, lean forward, "humping" your back, and bring elbows to the front. Hold five seconds.

Adapted from Friedeberger, J. (1992) *Office Yoga: Tackling Tension with Simple Stretches You Can Do at Your Desk.* San Francisco: Thorsons SF.

Humor and Playfulness in the Workplace

GOAL

▶ To capitalize on humor as a way of motivating and helping participants become more effective in technology staff development programs.

FOCUS QUESTION

▶ How can we encourage each other to use humor to generate creative thinking? Find solutions to vexing problems?

STRATEGY

1. Share the following information:
   Laughing helps us relax by decreasing adrenaline and other stress hormones. When we belly laugh, we also increase the body's beta endorphins (morphinelike painkillers). Thus, laughter eases pain. Laughter also may ease conditions such as hypertension, heart disease, cancer, autoimmune disease, and anxiety disorders. Humor paints a sensory picture.

   A funny story helps you remember the points and increases retention of material. Humor helps us see things more playfully.
   Lesson: Being foolish and taking risks are important to our well-being and effectiveness.

2. Then ask the following question: How many of you have Humor Deficit Disorder (HDD or lack of laughter)? Symptoms include:
   a. taking yourself too seriously   **c.** not living in the present
   b. desensitizing yourself   **d.** defensiveness

3. Then get the group to brainstorm ways of increasing humor in the technology staff development program. Get them to consider the following examples:
   a. Keep a humor file about technology. Tear out things that amuse you. Share them with others in the group and make HyperCard or LinkWay Live stacks.
   b. Adorn the bulletin board with cartoons and quips that relate to technology.
   c. Learn to laugh at yourself and your mistakes in every session.
   d. Help other people laugh at themselves.
   e. Read joke books every day. Share them with each other.

DISCUSSION QUESTIONS

▶ How can humor give you a new perspective about technology?
▶ Why does humor give you a fresh way of looking at old issues?
▶ How can humor be helpful to your well-being and effectiveness?

REFERENCE

Adapted from Shouse, D. "Laughing Matters," *Star Magazine*, May 9, 1993.

Is This Sick Humor or What?

GOAL

▶ To illustrate humorous ways of thinking about computer viruses and to begin a learning activity in a humorous fashion.

FOCUS QUESTION

▶ Have you heard about these new computer viruses?

STRATEGY

1. Select several of these virus jokes to share with participants:

PAUL REVERE VIRUS: This revolutionary virus does not horse around. It warns you of impending hard-disk attack—once if by LAN, twice if by C.

POLITICALLY CORRECT VIRUS: Refers to itself as an "electronic microorganism."

ROSS PEROT VIRUS: Activates every component in your system, just before the whole thing quits.

OPRAH WINFREY VIRUS: Your 200MB hard drive suddenly shrinks to 80MB, and then slowly expands back to 200MB.

TED TURNER VIRUS: Colorizes your monochrome monitor.

DAN QUAYLE VIRUS: Their is sumthing rong with your computer, ewe just can't figyour out watt.

GOVERNMENT ECONOMIST VIRUS: Nothing works, but all your diagnostic software says everything is fine.

ADAM & EVE VIRUS: Takes a couple bytes out of your Apple.

OLLIE NORTH VIRUS: Turns your printer into a document shredder.

NIKE VIRUS: Just Does IT!

LAPD VIRUS: It claims it feels threatened by the other files on you PC and erases them in self-defense.

JIMMY HOFFA VIRUS: Nobody can find it.

AIRLINE VIRUS: You're in New Orleans, but your data is in Greenville, North Carolina.

2. Allow participants to share others or create their own.

DISCUSSION QUESTIONS

▶ Have you heard a virus joke?
▶ What does this kind of humor say about people who use and like technology?
▶ Why is humor important in the technology staff development program?

REFERENCE

Author unknown, Internet, 1993.

The Edison Effect

GOAL

▶ To teach technology staff development participants that they have geniuslike powers when they concentrate their thinking in group problem-solving activities.

FOCUS QUESTION

▶ How can we maximize our problem-solving skills?

STRATEGY

1. Relate the following story:

   Thomas A. Edison said his secret of success was his ability to apply his "physical and mental energies to one problem incessantly." Edison had over 1,300 patents. Edison looked for solutions to technical problems by drawing on his creative "twilight phases." A technique that he perfected was falling asleep by standing up with a metal ball in his hand. When he dozed off, the ball would fall and wake him up and he immediately wrote down all images, words, and ideas in his mind. Researchers now think he was drawing on his powers to create a state in his brain called *theta activity*. There are four states: (1) Alpha—state of waking relaxation, (2) Beta—state of high-intensity attention, (3) Delta—pattern of brain in deep dreamless sleep or profound meditation, and (4) Theta—state of your brain when you're dreaming or in a near-sleep, "twilight" state.

2. Ask the group how and where they draw on their mental energies. List these techniques for others to discuss.

DISCUSSION QUESTIONS

▶ What can technology staff development teams and team leaders learn from this story?
▶ How much time are teachers and administrators given to think about creative problem solving about school improvement—specifically, transforming education with the emerging technologies?
▶ How many potential Edisons do we have in our leadership ranks?

REFERENCE

Adapted from Millard, A.J. (1990). *Edison and the Business of Innovation*. Baltimore: Johns Hopkins University Press.

Imagine That!

GOAL

▶ To show the group that anything is possible and to encourage technology staff development participants to increase their imagination.

FOCUS QUESTION

▶ What kind of creativity does it take to teach and learn with technology?

STRATEGY

1. Announce that you will step through an 8¹/₂-by-11-inch piece of paper by pulling it over your head.

2. Proceed to ask the participants how many people think you can do this.

3. First, fold the piece of paper in half lengthwise, cutting it with scissors from one side, then from the other. When this is finished, make a long cut along the folded edge, from the first snip to the last. Finally, unfold the paper, open it up, step into it, and pull it over your head. See illustration below:

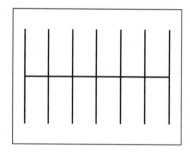

4. Explain to participants that many of them felt that you could not step through the piece of paper because they are stifled by conventional thinking.

DISCUSSION QUESTIONS

▶ What implications does this activity have for our technology staff development program?
▶ Can we exhibit this much creativity when it comes to using the emerging technologies to transform education?
▶ What can we do to increase our creativity when we use the emerging technologies?

Leadership

GOAL
► To explore the meaning of leadership in technology staff development programs.

FOCUS QUESTIONS
► How should leadership be defined?
► How should technology leadership be defined?

STRATEGY
Review and then circulate the "Leadership Axioms" list (see next page).

1. Allow participants to discuss the meaning of leadership in technology staff development programs. Specifically, address these two questions:
   a. What is the role of the administrator as a technology leader?
   b. What is the relationship between leaders and team members in technology-related staff development programs?

2. Direct participants to come up with their own axioms which reflect their beliefs about leadership.

3. Allow participants to synthesize these axioms into a profile of leadership.

DISCUSSION QUESTIONS
► If you had to walk around with one axiom on your forehead, what would it say?
► Which axiom or axioms best reflect your concept of leadership?
► Of what value are axioms to technology leaders?
► What should be the basic axioms of leadership in your technology staff development program?

Leadership Axioms

▶ Authority does not make you a leader, it gives you the opportunity to be one.

▶ Leadership depends on the ability to make people want to follow.

▶ Good leaders not only know where they are going, but they can persuade other people to come along on the journey.

▶ Good leadership is the art of getting average people to do excellent work.

▶ You cannot lead where you have not gone.

▶ The problem of leadership is that it is hard to tell if people are following or chasing you.

▶ A leader cannot be effective in giving orders without being able to receive orders.

▶ Master your ability to focus and you will master your ability to lead.

▶ A leader is a person who has been empowered to empower others.

▶ The difference between having an idea and following through on an idea is effective leadership.

▶ *Good* leaders inspire others to have faith in them while *great* leaders inspire others to have confidence in themselves.

▶ People become what you *encourage* them to be—not what you require them to be.

▶ You cannot teach something you don't know. In other words, you cannot come back from where you haven't been.

▶ Authority is not the same as leadership.

▶ Effective leaders find pathways, while others find excuses.

▶ Following the leader is easier than leading the followers.

▶ You become a leader when you cause people to share the rewards, as well as the failures.

▶ Two kinds of persons never become leaders: one who cannot do what he or she is told and the other is one who cannot do anything unless he or she is told.

▶ You cannot lead if you have not followed.

▶ Effective leaders build bridges while ineffective ones build fences.

▶ People who will not follow and cannot lead should get out of the way.

Using Metaphors to Communicate

GOAL

▶ To show the power of metaphors as a tool to communicate, solve problems, and discover new insights when using technology.

FOCUS QUESTIONS

▶ What is a metaphor?

▶ How can metaphors help us communicate with each other when integrating technology into teaching and learning?

STRATEGY

1. Relate the following to participants:

A metaphor is a figure of speech in which a term is transferred from the object it ordinarily designates to an object it may designate by comparison or analogy. Metaphors help people find similarity between ideas. Most metaphors are visual. Thus, if you can use a metaphor to help people remember, they're less likely to forget. A way to begin thinking about metaphors is by asking questions. Listen to the following:

▶ How is using a computer like flying an airplane?

▶ How is experimenting with new technologies like exploring a jungle?

▶ How is learning a new way of teaching like giving birth to a child?

2. Here is a list of potential metaphors that you could use when thinking about the emerging technologies and the technology staff development program.

Cooking a meal	Conducting an orchestra	Fighting a fire
Giving a speech	Selling a product	Raising a child
Playing Baseball	Planting a garden	Saving money
Discovering a new planet	Flying in a rocket ship	Getting married
Looking for a job	Writing a story	Getting a divorce

3. Now take a problem that you have studied in the emerging technologies and develop a metaphor around it. See if the metaphor helps you understand the problem better.

4. Explain these examples to other participants in your group.

DISCUSSION QUESTIONS

▶ How can metaphors enhance your understanding of a problem?

▶ How can using metaphors help you become a better technology leader?

REFERENCE

Adapted from von Oech, R. (1986). *A Kick in the Seat of the Pants—Using Your Explorer, Artist, Judge, & Warrior to Be More Creative*. New York: HarperCollins.

Who Said That?

GOAL

▶ To explore the origin of quotes or misquotes when thinking about the emerging technologies and technology leadership.

FOCUS QUESTIONS

▶ How do quotes originate?

▶ How can technology leaders and teams use quotes to articulate their beliefs and opinions?

▶ What quotes best reflect your opinions about technology?

STRATEGY

Review the summary sheet entitled "Who Said That?" (see next page) to familiarize yourself with the story about quotes and misquotes. Then:

1. allow participants to review quotes.

2. allow participants to select or make up their own quotes that they wish to use when speaking to others about the technology staff development program.

3. have participants select the most appropriate quote which illustrates their passion and belief in the emerging technologies as tools to transform education.

DISCUSSION QUESTIONS

▶ Why do we use quotes?

▶ Why are quotations a powerful way of communicating?

▶ Why do we misquote so routinely?

▶ What quotations best reflect the power of technology to transform education?

REFERENCE

Adapted from Keyes, R. (1992). *Nice Guys Finish Seventh: False Phrases, Spurious Sayings and Familiar Misquotations*. New York: HarperCollins.

Who Said That?

▶ Did Harry Truman say "If you can't stand the heat, get out of the kitchen"?
Not originally, he got this comment from his old friend Harry Vaughan.

▶ Did you know that a number of impressive quotations are actually misquotations?
Many of our best-known sayings, phrases, and comments are inaccurate.

Leo Durocher, for example, never said "Nice guys finish last."

General William Tecumseh Sherman never said "War is hell." He really said "There is many a boy here today who looks on war as all glory, but boys, it is all hell."

Charles E. Wilson never said "What's good for General Motors is good for the country." He actually said ". . .for years, I thought that what was good for our country was good for General Motors and vice versa."

▶ Putting words in the mouths of famous people works best when people are dead.
For example:

"Taxation without representation is tyranny!"

"Give me liberty or give me death!"

"We must all hang together, or most assuredly we shall all hang separately."

These quotes were attributed to James Otis, Patrick Henry, and Benjamin Franklin long after their deaths. Were these words theirs? You better check it out!

▶ Words carry more weight if they're attributed to someone famous.

P.T. Barnum didn't say "There is a sucker born every minute, but none of them die."

W.C. Fields said "Never give a sucker an even break," but the writer-gambler Wilson Mizner used that phrase long before Fields.

▶ Many quotes are misquotes.
Abraham Lincoln is routinely misquoted. Remember this famous quote: "You can fool all of the people some of the time; you can even fool some of the people all of the time; but you can't fool all of the people all of the time." Most historians don't believe Lincoln said that.

Adapted from Keyes, R. (1992). *Nice Guys Finish Seventh: False Phrases, Spurious Sayings and Familiar Misquotations*. New York: HarperCollins.

Pearls of Technology Wisdom

GOAL

▶ To explore the wisdom that each of us have learned about technology.

FOCUS QUESTIONS

▶ What have you learned about technology in the past few years?

▶ How can you pass on what you have learned to others?

STRATEGY

1. Share the following with participants:

   The young, middle age, and elderly have gleaned a few bits of wisdom in the time that they have spent on Earth. Here are some:

   ▶ There's no elevator to success. You have to take the stairs.—age 48

   ▶ The best tranquilizer is a clear conscience.—age 76

   ▶ You can love four girls at the same time.—age 9

   Now here are some that relate to technology and technology leadership:

   ▶ The time to read the instructions is before you take the computer out of the box.—age 36

   ▶ Computers are so nearly human that they can do things without using any intelligence.—age 96

   ▶ The great thing about computers is that you can use a lot of words that you don't know how to spell.—age 16

2. Allow participants to come up with their own pearls of technology wisdom.

3. Have participants write and compile their own electronic book of technology wisdom to pass on to future technology staff development teams.

DISCUSSION QUESTIONS

▶ Why are these pearls of technology wisdom so powerful?

▶ What pearls best reflect what you have learned about technology?

REFERENCE

Adapted from H. Jackson Brown, Jr. (1992). *Live and Learn and Pass it On*. Nashville, TN: Ruthledge Hill Press.

Communicate by Negotiating

GOAL
▶ To help establish or publicize expectations of technology trainer and participants.

FOCUS QUESTIONS
▶ What are participant expectations of this technology training session?
▶ What are trainer expectations of this technology training session?

STRATEGY
A common problem of many training sessions is that the trainer and participants have two sets of expectations. When the trainer is headed in one direction and participants are headed in another, you can expect trouble.

To deal with this situation, the trainer should deal with goals and expectations at the outset of the training session.

1. The trainer might say: "On the flip chart or slide, you can see the major goals that I have established for the training session." (Read them and discuss them.)

2. "Now that you know my goals, what are two or three expectations that you have of this workshop?" (Write them down on the flip chart or computer/LCD panel.)

3. At this point, the trainer should begin to negotiate with participants and try to mesh his or her goals with participant needs. Try to accommodate needs, but it is preferable to indicate what can be done in the workshop and what can better be dealt with at another time.

4. Leave the negotiated goals and expectations in full view and refer to them during the training session to ensure that everyone knows what concepts have been dealt with and what upcoming concepts will be covered.

5. During closure of the training session, review the goals and expectations.

DISCUSSION QUESTIONS
▶ How well did we accomplish our mutually agreed-upon goals?
▶ What did we accomplish?
▶ What didn't we accomplish?
▶ Where do we go from here?

Let's Take a Break!

GOAL

► To set the stage for breaks and adhering to a time schedule with humor and dignity.

FOCUS QUESTION

► How can I get you (participants) to come back on time after taking a break?

STRATEGY

A common problem for technology trainers is getting participants to return on time. When they don't, the training schedule gets derailed and you can find yourself in trouble. Even worse, they may interrupt your presentation.

Threats about tardiness are rarely acceptable. What typically happens is that the trainer ignores the behavior or frets over the unacceptable behavior without acknowledging the irritation to his or her audience.

To deal with potentially unacceptable tardiness in a humorous fashion, try the following:

1. Instruct people about the break.

2. Indicate how much time is to be allotted.

3. Then determine a consequence that will be very embarrassing to participants in a good-natured fashion.
Some examples:
   ► "We will come back at ___ a.m. Those who are late must come to the front and sing a song (e.g., school's fight song, National Anthem, etc.).
   ► "We will come back at ___ a.m. Those who are late must come to the front and recite an original poem. For example:
   > "Roses are red,
   > Violets are blue,
   > I was late,
   > So kick me with your shoe."
   ► We will come back at ___p.m. Those who are late will find the door locked (e.g., temporarily hold the door shut while latecomers try to come back into the room).
   ► Those who come back on time will be eligible for a prize (e.g., provide some small token such as pin, book, etc.). Those who arrive late will not be eligible. The drawing will occur at ___a.m.

NOTE: When done with humor and lightheartedness, these behavior-consequence situations used at break time can generate substantial humor. When done in a mean-spirited fashion, the group will not find the trainer's actions amusing.

DISCUSSION QUESTION

► None necessary.

Technology Jargon

GOAL

▶ To understand the implications of jargon when used in a technology staff development program.

FOCUS QUESTIONS

▶ Is the trainer presenting his or her message in a clear and concise way?

▶ Does the trainer have an obligation to present materials in such a way that they can be easily understood by all participants?

STRATEGY

1. Each group is given a set of directions which are lengthy and complex.

2. Each group takes their sentence and turns it into a clear, jargon-free sentence while still maintaining the same meaning.

3. Then each group exchanges sentences and tries to decipher what the original sentence said.

4. Possible examples include:

> "Some actions, such as saving a document, can't be reversed. In this case, Undo changes to Can't Undo and is dimmed on menus."

> Translation: *Once you save it, that's it!*

> "Numerous repetitive hand-finger actions in computer keyboarding exercises could lead to long-term impairment of normal physical hand movement and could eventually lead to permanent damage (carpel tunnel syndrome). Rest at regular intervals is recommended."

> Translation: *If you hit your fingers too much on the keyboard, it may hurt your fingers or wrist—permanently! Don't forget to take a break!"*

DISCUSSION QUESTIONS

▶ Does jargon have a place when we are trying to communicate to the general public? Other administrators? Colleagues?

▶ Does jargon impact people differently when we are conveying our message electronically?

▶ Do educators need to be aware of the wide variety of jargon that is being spawned by the emerging technologies?

Listen to What's Coming Out of Your Mouth!

GOAL

▶ To explore the power of a trainer's verbal communication in technology training sessions and the dramatic impact on participants' performance and attitude.

FOCUS QUESTIONS

▶ What are some basic definitions and examples of trainer verbal communication skills?

▶ How can you (as a technology trainer) become more aware of what you say and how those words impact participants?

STRATEGY

Review the summary sheet "Verbal Communication Skills" (see next page) to familiarize yourself with the six verbal communication skills. Then:

1. videotape or audiotape one of your training sessions.

2. look for actual examples of the six verbal cues skills.

3. explain the purpose of the taping session to participants.

4. review the videotape.

5. determine which skills were used effectively or ineffectively.

6. determine which skills were not observed whatsoever.

7. create a plan that identifies which behaviors you want to monitor and improve over the next few training sessions.

NOTE: This activity must be an ongoing practice by technology trainers. Selecting one behavior to work on at a time is advisable rather than looking at all six verbal communication skills at one time.

DISCUSSION QUESTION

▶ None necessary.

Verbal Communication Skills

TRAINER VERBAL BEHAVIOR	EXAMPLES
1. Accepting/Expressing Emotions—expressing, clarifying, or recalling past feelings	"I know how you feel."
2. Positive Reinforcement—praising or encouraging	"That's a good example."
3. Building—making statements that buttress, develop, or elaborate on responses	"Last week, Mary said that the emerging technologies were . . ."
4. Questioning—seeking information from others	"Who else remembers what we said about the emerging technologies?"
5. Direction Giving—giving directions, commands, or orders with which an individual is expected to comply	"Please read the following handout."
6. Criticism—changing unacceptable behavior to acceptable behavior	"We need to be quiet for a few minutes for this activity."

What's Your Body Doing?

GOAL

▶ To explore the trainer's power of nonverbal communication in technology training sessions and the dramatic impact that it has on participants' performance and attitudes.

FOCUS QUESTIONS

▶ What are some basic definitions and examples of technology trainer nonverbal communication?

▶ How can you (the technology trainer) become more aware of what you are saying nonverbally and how it impacts participants?

STRATEGY

Review the summary sheet (see next page) to familiarize yourself with the 11 nonverbal communication skills. Then:

1. videotape or audiotape one of your training sessions.

2. look for actual examples of the 11 verbal skills.

3. explain to participants the purpose of the taping session.

4. review the videotape to analyze the various 11 verbal skills.

5. determine which skills were used effectively and ineffectively.

6. determine which skills where not observed whatsoever.

7. write down a plan which identifies which behaviors you want to monitor and improve over the next few training sessions.

NOTE: This activity must be an ongoing practice by trainers. Selecting only a few behaviors to work on at a time is advisable rather than looking at all 11 nonverbal communication skills at one time.

DISCUSSION QUESTION

▶ None necessary.

Nonverbal Communication Skills

NONVERBAL BEHAVIOR	POSSIBLE EXAMPLE
1. Eye Contact—looking into the other's eyes (gaze)	looks directly into eyes
2. Gestures—behaviors which buttress verbal message; meaningful	holds up two fingers to emphasize second point
3. Mannerisms—physical movements that are mindless behaviors; little relationship to what is being said	rubs nose continually
4. Touching—physical contact	places hand on back
5. Facial Expressions—messages sent with eyebrows, cheeks, nose, lips, tongue, etc.	frowns while talking
6. Posture—standing, sitting, slouching, stooping, etc.	sits on edge of table while giving example
7. Energy Level—enthusiasm, speed, volume, etc.	picks up pace and moves faster
8. Use of Space—arrangement	chairs are placed around computers in circular fashion to enhance group interaction
9. Silence—absence of sound	three-second lapse after stating question
10. Travel—movement within the designated space	travels to each technology team
11. Use of Time—how time is spent	spends 90 percent of time on one topic while spending only 10 percent on next topic

Tell Me the Bad News First!

GOAL

▶ To explore reasons why people want to hear the negative before they hear the positive—especially when it relates to technology.

FOCUS QUESTIONS

▶ Why do people have a natural inclination to hear negative things?

▶ How does this human reaction impact the productivity of technology team cohesiveness?

STRATEGY

1. Share the following information:
No matter how much people may think they crave good news over bad, subconsciously they don't —unless it is sex. That's what experimentation has led Felica Pratto, a Stanford University psychologist, to conclude. Pratto believes that a person's mental automatic processing system gives more attention to negative stimuli than to positive ones. She labels this behavior *automatic vigilance* and thinks it is an evolutionary adaptation that helps protect individuals from danger. Only notions related to reproduction, like babies and sex, seem to have the same power to attract our subconscious attention as do negative stimuli. In tests, people pay greater attention to negative information, believing that it may protect them from immediate harm.

2. Get participants to discuss automatic vigilance and its implications for slowing or preventing the transformation of schools with the emerging technologies.

3. Have participants discuss strategies for understanding and dealing with automatic vigilance.

DISCUSSION QUESTIONS

▶ What does this information suggest about groups when they hear information?

▶ What does this say about teams when they process information about positive and negative information?

▶ What examples can you provide about automatic vigilance in work and your family?

▶ What does "automatic vigilance" tell us about how to help people prepare for technology staff development programs?

REFERENCE

Adapted from "Subconscious Is Attracted More to Negative Stimuli," (November 9, 1992), *Kansas City Star*.

And Now for Our Next Guest

GOAL
▶ To welcome outside technology consultants in a creative way.

FOCUS QUESTION
▶ How can we make our technology consultants feel welcome in novel ways?

STRATEGY

1. Request a copy of the technology speaker or facilitator's vita well in advance of the training session.

2. Divide the vita into several sections that merit sharing with participants.

3. Select three or four people who will share the information from the vita.

4. Have them position themselves in different locations in the room.

5. When the guest speaker is about to be introduced, say, "We have been doing lots of research on our distinguished guest. There are several people in our audience who can tell you about some of the great accomplishments of our speaker."

6. Then designate those people to provide information about the speaker and allow them to share their knowledge with the rest of the participants.

DISCUSSION QUESTION
▶ None necessary.

Tales from Technology Hell

GOAL

▶ To develop an awareness that almost everyone has glitches with technology, and that these experiences can wreak havoc in our lives.

FOCUS QUESTIONS

▶ Has technology (specifically your computer) nearly driven you over the edge?
▶ How can we hate what we dearly love?

STRATEGY

1. Relate the following:
Almost every one of us has had a harrowing experience with our computers. Sweaty palms, churning stomach, and night sweats are not uncommon for those of us who have had our hard disk crash unexpectedly. It is important for us to talk and share our nightmares and fears about computers. It is only natural. Rather than ignore these experiences, it is therapeutic for us to talk about them, laugh about them, and share them with others.

2. Assign the following activities:
OPTION #1: Write a description of your horror story with computers.
OPTION #2: Draw a picture of your most nightmarish experience with your computer (drawing can be hand- or computer-generated).

3. Allow participants to share stories or pictures with each other.

4. Allow the group to vote on the best story or picture.

5. Offer an inexpensive prize for the best story.

DISCUSSION QUESTIONS

▶ Why is it healthy to discuss anger and frustration when using technology?
▶ What are people's greatest fears of using computers and the emerging technologies?
▶ Is it natural for people to have these fears and frustrations?

Fax It Fast!

GOAL

▶ To use a "fun type" story to stimulate creativity in the technology staff development program.

FOCUS QUESTION

▶ How close are we to a paperless society?

STRATEGY

1. Relate the following information:

   Paperless workplace? Think again. Major companies are receiving 43 percent more faxes this year (1993) than last, according to a Gallup poll commissioned by Pitney Bowes. The paperless office that was predicted by computer companies is not here and it is not close. The average *Fortune 500* company gets 428 pages a day by fax, versus 300 a day last year (1992). A company sends an average 49 documents totaling 260 pages a day—up 41 percent from last year (1992). About 70 percent of companies say they have no policy or guidelines to control fax usage.

2. Suggested activities:

   ▶ Determine how many faxes are sent by your school.

   ▶ Determine how many are received.

   ▶ Determine what form or forms are used to send the fax. Are they official looking or humorous? Exchange formats with other participants.

   ▶ Determine if your school has a policy or guidelines which limits the amount of fax usage.

DISCUSSION QUESTIONS

▶ Should schools and organizations have a policy or guideline to control fax usage? Why or why not?

▶ What accounts for this new form of communication in the workplace?

REFERENCE

Adapted from "Fax Users Paper Offices," *USA Today* (May 18, 1993).

The Haves and Have-Nots

GOAL

▶ To make participants aware of who owns and uses computers by showing that even though computer use is rising, there still may be a growing discrepancy between those who have access to a computer and those who do not—the haves and have-nots.

FOCUS QUESTION

▶ Why is it important that educators recognize the importance of mastering computer skills and information about who owns computers today?

STRATEGY

1. Circulate "Who Owns a Computer?" (see next page).

2. Discuss the implications of this information for schools and parents.

3. What implications does this have for technology leaders?

DISCUSSION QUESTIONS

▶ Why is it important that we make sure all students have access to computers and the emerging technologies?

▶ Will the relationship of successful wage earners and computer ownership continue in the future?

▶ Do all students have an equal opportunity to learn computers skills in schools today?

▶ What must we do to ensure that the discrepancy between haves and have-nots does not continue?

REFERENCE

"Software Publishers Association Report," *Kansas City Star* (May 4, 1993) and *USA Today* (May 3, 1993).

Who Owns a Computer?

1. Computer owners are wealthier and better-educated than most people.

2. In almost every category of wealth and education, the spread is more than 2 to 1.

3. Twenty-seven percent of computer owners have incomes of $75,000 or more.

4. More than 50 percent of computer owners make more than $50,000.

5. More than 50 percent of computer owners have more than four years of college as compared with fewer than one-quarter of the general population who have four years of college.

6. The median time in front of the machine for computer owners is four hours a week.

7. For those computer owners who do any business at home, the median time jumps to 20 hours a week.

8. The percentage of top executives who use PCs regularly at work jumped from 42 percent in 1989 to 81 percent in 1993.

9. One in three children under the age of five have had experience with a computer.

"Software Publishers Association Report," *Kansas City Star* (May 4, 1993) and *USA Today* (May 3, 1993).

Will You Please Be Quiet!

GOAL

▶ To get participants' attention with dignity and finesse.

FOCUS QUESTION

▶ How can I get participants to quiet down without acting like a jerk?

STRATEGY

A common problem for technology trainers is getting participants' attention to start a new activity or getting their attention immediately after a high-energy activity. Effective trainers deal with this situation with forethought—with dignity, finesse, and sometimes humor.

To deal effectively with this kind of behavior, the technology trainer needs to experiment with a number of strategies that fit his or her personality and the personality of the group.

1. Instruct people that there will be a number of activities and you will need to establish some forms of communication when you need their attention.

2. Then try one the following options:

    a. Hold a closed fist when you (the trainer) wish to speak.

    b. Hold up two fingers to start small-group discussion. Hold up four fingers when you wish the small groups to stop.

    c. Blow a whistle. Once to start group. Twice to stop group.

    d. Play music to signal beginning and ending of group work.

    e. Hold up cards (e.g., green card for *talk* and red card to signal *stop talking*). Give participants colored card (e.g., yellow) which indicates that they wish to talk or need to ask a question.

NOTE: By focusing on the process and not personalizing the rules, most adults will abide by the rules. Technology trainers should not use these strategies to dominate or punish individual behavior. Viewed as rules to enhance the training session, most participants will recognize the positive, constructive nature of your strategy and appreciate your grasp of group leadership.

DISCUSSION QUESTION

▶ None necessary.

Warm Up

GOAL

▶ To help technology team members get acquainted, reacquainted, or simply talk to get warmed up to the work at hand.

FOCUS QUESTION

▶ How can we facilitate technology teams to feel comfortable about themselves and others?

STRATEGY

A common problem when groups are first getting acquainted or starting to work is to get in the mood. Try the following strategy.

TAKE A LOOK INTO THE FUTURE

Directions: Take about three or four minutes to answer each of the following questions. Imagine that you are living in the year 2020. Discuss your answers with each other.

1. What does USD # _____ look like?

2. What changes, factors, variables have impacted your school since the early 1990s?

3. How are students learning today?

4. What changes have been the most dramatic since the 1990s?

DISCUSSION QUESTIONS

▶ What did most of you think about—in terms of change?

▶ What kinds of technology was being used in the year 2020? How was it being used? How does it compare to the technology of the 1990s?

STAFF DEVELOPMENT AND THE EMERGING TECHNOLOGIES

Bailey, G. & Lumley, D. (1994). *Technology Staff Development Programs: A Leadership Sourcebook for School Administrators*. New York: Scholastic.

STAGE 1: PREPARING FOR CHANGE AND UNDERSTANDING TECHNOLOGY STAFF DEVELOPMENT PROGRAMS

Abram, M. & Bernstein, H. (1989). *Future Stuff*. New York: Penguin Books.

Abram, M. & Bernstein, H. (1989). *More Future Stuff*. New York: Penguin Books.

Barker, J.A. (1992). *Future Edge—Discovering the New Paradigms of Success*. New York: William Morrow.

Berger, C.F. & Carlson, E.A. (1988). Increasing Teacher Access to Ongoing Computer Training. *Technological Horizons in Education, 15* (9), 64–68.

Bruder, I. (1989). "New Ideas for Professional Development." *Electronic Learning, 9*(3), 27.

Caldwell, S.D. (Ed.) (1989). *Staff Development: A Handbook of Effective Practices*. Oxford, OH: National Staff Development Council.

Carrier, C. A., Glenn A.D. & Sales, G.C. (1985). "A Two Level Program for Training Teachers to Use Computers in the Classroom," *Educational Technology, 25* (10), 18-23.

Dillon-Peterson, B. (Ed.) (1981). *Staff Development/Organization Development*. Washington, D.C.: ASCD.

Joyce B. & Showers, B. (1980). "Improving Inservice Training: The Messages of Research." *Educational Leadership, 37* (5), 369–385.

Joyce B. & Showers, B. (1988). *Student Achievement Through Staff Development*. New York: Longman Press.

Joyce, B. (Ed.) (1990). *Changing School Culture Through Staff Development*. Washington, D.C.: ASCD.

Kearsley, G. (1990). *Computers for Educational Administrators—Leadership in the Information-Age*. Norwood, NJ: Ablex.

Perelman, L.J. (1987). *Technology and Transformation of Schools*. Washington, D.C.: National School Boards Association.

Perelman, L.J. (1992). *School's Out: Hyperlearning, the New Technology, and the End of Education*. New York: William Morrow.

Roszack, T. (1986). *The Cult of Information: The Folklore of Computers and the True Art of Thinking*. New York: Pantheon Books.

Sheingold, K., and Tucker, M.S. (1990). *Restructuring for Learning with Technology*. New York: Center for Technology in Education, Bank Street College of Education, with National Center on Education and the Economy.

Sparks, G.M. (1983). "Synthesis of Research on Staff Development for Effective Teaching." *Educational Leadership, 41* (3), 65–72.

Toffler, A. (1970). *Future Shock.* New York: Random House.

Toffler, A. (1980). *Third Wave.* New York: William Morrow.

Toffler, A. (1990). *Powershift: Knowledge, Wealth, and Violence at the Edge of the 21st Century,* New York: Bantam.

STAGE 2: PLANNING TECHNOLOGY STAFF DEVELOPMENT PROGRAMS

Apple Computer, Inc. (1991). *Teaching, Learning, & Technology—A Planning Guide.* Cupertino, CA: Apple Computer Inc.

Bailey, G. & Lumley, D. (September 1991). "How to Plan Productive Committee Meetings." *NASSP-Tips for Principals.*

Batey, A. (ed.) (1988). *Planning for Computers in Education.* location Northwest Regional Education Laboratory.

Bracey, G. (1990). "Education Still Not Looking at the Big Picture." *Electronic Learning, 9* (80), 20–21.

Covey, S.R. (1989). *The 7 Habits of Highly Effective People: Powerful Lessons in Personal Change.* New York: Fireside.

Dede, C. (1989). "Planning Guidelines for Emerging Instructional Technologies." *Educational Technology, 29* (4), 7–12.

Hughes, B. (1990). "Long-Range Planning." *Electronic Learning, 10* (3), 10.

Lumley, D. & Bailey, G. (1993). *Planning for Technology—A Guidebook for School Administrators.* New York: Scholastic.

Nadler, G. & Hibino, S. (1990). *Breakthrough Thinking: Why We Must Change the Way We Solve Problems and the Seven Principles to Achieve This.* Rocklin, CA: Prima.

Senge, P. (1990). *The Fifth Discipline—The Art & Practice of the Learning Organization.* New York: Doubleday.

United Way Strategic Institute (1989). *What Lies Ahead: Countdown to the 21st Century,* Alexandria, VA: United Way of America.

Wolff, M. (1992). *Where We Stand—Can America Make It in the Global Race for Wealth, Health, and Happiness?* New York: Bantam.

STAGE 3: IMPLEMENTING TECHNOLOGY STAFF DEVELOPMENT PROGRAMS

Blohowiak, D.W. (1993). *Mavericks! How to Lead Your Staff to Think Like Einstein, Create Like da Vinci, and Invent Like Edison.* Homewood, Illinois: Business One Irwin.

Bracey, G.W. (1992). "Computers and Cooperative Learning." *Electronic Learning, 11* (5), 14.

D'Ignazio, F. (1991). "Integrating the Work Environment of the 1990s Into Today's Classrooms." *T.H.E. Journal, 18* (11), 95.

Kinnaman, D. (1990). "Staff Development: How to Build Your Winning Team." *Technology & Learning, 11* (2), 24–30.

Schrage, M. (1990). *Shared Minds: The New Technologies of Collaboration*. New York: Random House.

Sher, B. & Gottlieb, A. (1989). *TeamWorks! Building Support Groups that Guarantee Success*. New York: Warner.

von Oech, R. (1986). *A Kick in the Seat of the Pants—Using Your Explorer, Artist, Judge, & Warrior to Be More Creative*. New York: Harper Perennial.

von Oech, R. (1990). *A Wack in the Side of the Head—How You Can Be More Creative*. New York: Warner Books.

STAGE 4: INSTITUTIONALIZING TECHNOLOGY STAFF DEVELOPOMENT PROGRAMS

Armstrong, T. (1993). *7 Kinds of Smart: Identifying and Developing Your Many Intelligences*. New York: Plume.

Gardner, H. (1983). *Frames of Mind: The Theory of Multiple Intelligences*. New York: Basic Books.

Newman, F.M. (1991). "Linking Restructuring to Authentic Student Assessment." *Phi Delta Kappan*, 72 (6), 458–463.

STAGE 5: SPECIAL ACTIVITIES FOR SITUATIONS AND TRAINERS

Boone, M. (1991). *Leadership and the Computer—Top Executives Reveal How They Personally Use Computers to Communicate, Coach, Convince, and Compete*. Rocklin, CA: Prima.

Kelly, R. (1992). *The Power of Leadership—How to Create Leaders People Want to Follow and Followers Who Lead Themselves*. New York: Doubleday.

Wurman, R.S. (1989). *Information Anxiety: What to Do When Information Doesn't Tell You What You Need to Know*. New York: Bantam Books.

Dr. Gerald D. Bailey is a professor of education in the department of educational administration and a technology consultant at Kansas State University, Manhattan, Kansas.

Jerry is a former classroom teacher, supervising demonstration teacher, and university supervisor. He is the author of several technology leadership articles and the coauthor of *Planning for Technology* (1993), *Technology Staff Development Programs* (1994) and *Technology-Based Learning Methods* (preparing).

Dr. Gwen L. Bailey is a leadership consultant in Manhattan, Kansas. Gwen is a former alternative school teacher in the public schools and grants coordinator at Kansas State University. She is the author of several articles and books on adult education and leadership.